MARY STUART, QUEEN OF SCOTS

THE STORY OF
THE MARYS

BY
GRACE HUMPHREY

ILLUSTRATED BY
EDWARD SHENTON

THE PENN PUBLISHING
COMPANY PHILADELPHIA
1928

To my Mother whose
name is
M A R Y

CONTENTS

ILLUSTRATIONS

The Story of the Marys

HOW THIS BOOK CAME TO BE

"GRANDFATHER," asked Mary suddenly breaking a long silence, "how'd they happen to name me Mary?"

"I named you, my dear," was his smiling reply. "When you were only a few hours old you were carried in to see us and this message came with you—'Tell Father he's to name her.' In half a minute more it was done, though of course you weren't christened till later. But I didn't hesitate about your name."

"I'm glad it was you, Grandfather. But why'd you choose Mary?"

"It's your grandmother's name, you know. Even as a teensy-weensy baby you looked like her."

He opened his watch, gazed at the picture of the Mary there, then at the eager girl before him and nodded his head.

"Yes, you're very like her, my dear—the same shaped face, the same big eyes, and the soft fluffiness of your hair. I remember saying to your grandmother, 'She shall be named Mary with the hope that she'll always look like you.'"

"And I do, everyone says. I'm glad I look like her since I have her name."

"So am I, Mary. But the day you came to us I wished for more than that. I wanted you to look like her, it's true, and grow up to be as beautiful as she is. But still more I wished that you might be as beautiful in character—loving and patient and gentle. That's what makes your grandmother so lovely, you see, the beauty and strength of her character shining out in her face. And that's my wish for you. I want you to have more than her name—or rather because you have that, I want the other gifts to be added unto you."

" Yes, Grandfather, I think I understand," Mary said very slowly, " kind and unselfish and being thoughtful for others and helping when I can, so that your hopes can all come true. But tell me, are all the Marys named for their grandmothers—Aunt Mary and the housemaid next door and little Mary Kingston in my class at school? "

" For a grandmother, for an aunt or friend. I suppose there isn't any other name so popular as Mary. Some girls are called that because it's so beautiful a word. Just say it over slowly, Mary, Mary, and see how lovely the sound is. And some girls have the name for some great woman ——"

" Like the Georges, Grandfather, named for Washington and not for their uncles or fathers? "

" Yes. For nearly two thousand years the name's been given to hundreds and thousands of girls in every land, always with the hope, I suppose, just as we hoped for you, that this particular Mary would grow up to be like some of the great women who've borne the name."

" Why, have the Marys been specially famous? "

" Oh yes. Some of them did great things for the world, very quietly or in a showy way that made them famous. Some sat on thrones and ruled over many people. Some ruled as wisely—over home and children. Some worked for the common people. So many, many Marys in the world's hall of fame! So much they've done! It would make a long, long story."

"Grandfather," said Mary looking up at him eagerly, "tell me about them, these great and famous women who've had my name. For if I was really christened for my grandmother, because you wanted me to be like her," she went on soberly, "and she was named for some other Mary, and that person for another one way long ago, then don't I specially belong to all the Marys and they to me?"

"Yes," he agreed and told her the stories of some of the famous Marys of the world. To a gloomy, old palace in Scotland the two journeyed and across to sunny France. They drove through the Massachusetts hills by stage-coach, over a Virginia plantation inspecting fields and fences, and through real English country with its green lanes and hedgerows and gardens and fine old trees. They watched the stars from a closet window and made a discovery in a fashion magazine. They went to a far-away village in Asia Minor. They steamed up the Mississippi on a hospital boat. They saw a fête in the gardens at Versailles and a Wednesday evening party in a clerk's lodgings in the Inner Temple. Wonderful times they had together!

And here are the stories for you to share with Mary and her grandfather.

The Story of the Marys

THE ROYAL MARY

Mary Stuart, Queen of Scots: 1542–1587

MARY was crying.

A long and stately procession marched up the steep streets of Stirling in Scotland. The trumpets blew. Mary cried. The people shouted and crowded about the doors of the chapel in the historic old castle. A new ruler was to be crowned, a queen of Scots.

But Mary cried the more. She understood nothing of all that was taking place that coronation day. She was just nine months old. She was terrified when she heard the great organ and saw only strange faces, instead of her mother and her good nurse. She cried the whole time.

She was afraid of the cardinal in his red robes when he placed the crown on her head. She was afraid of the nobles who knelt before her, one after another, to kiss her wee hand as a sign of loyalty. About the scepter they bent her baby fingers. Round

11

her waist they girded the great sword that the fighting kings of Scotland used to wear. But she cried still more.

"That's an evil omen," people said, "if her reign begins in tears!"

Indeed this little Mary had troubles aplenty. Away in the south warring against the English, her father had died before she was a week old. This left her ruler of Scotland. It was not an easy country to govern, for it was split into two great parties of Catholic and Protestant. And at that time, nearly four hundred years ago, religion meant politics and plots and counterplots.

The baby queen had still another cause of trouble. Her mother was to be regent till she was old enough to reign. And her mother was both French and Catholic, facts very displeasing to the Scottish lords.

While Mary was still in her nurse's arms one of the great nobles of Scotland proposed that she marry his little son. The king of England, stout old Henry the eighth, wanted her to marry his son Edward and so end the wars between the two countries. But he made hard conditions. He insisted that Mary must go to school in England and that he must have a share in the government of Scotland. To this, of course, the proud Scotch parliament would never agree. The wedding plans were broken off and Henry sent another army against the little queen.

"We have no objection to Prince Edward," said the Scots.

"But a maid should be wooed with gentle courtesy and not with battles." So they asked the French king to send soldiers to help them against the English. To this plan he assented if Mary was promised in marriage to his son Francis.

The ships which brought his troops across the sea, flying the blue flag with the golden lilies, took the six-year-old queen back to France. A brave little girl and a Stuart, she left her mother without crying. For the regent must stay in Scotland, but wished her daughter to be educated in her old home.

You mustn't think, however, that Mary's schooling hadn't begun long before she started to Paris. She could already speak French as well as she could English. She had studied history and geography and Latin. She could embroider and weave tapestry.

As they crossed the Channel to France a dreadful storm overtook the ship that bore the queen and her four little maids of honor, each named Mary. When they landed the first thing they did was to go to church to give thanks for having escaped the dangers of the sea and the hands of the English. With royal honors they were received. As they rode to Paris prisoners in the towns they passed through were set free. How those men must have welcomed the child!

Francis, the dauphin, as the heir to the throne of France was called, was a pale, delicate, backward boy some months younger than Mary. They became friends at once. To be sure even if they hadn't loved each other they would have married. But Francis adored her. He agreed absolutely with his brother who cried, " You're the happiest of men to possess a creature of so much loveliness! "

The children had their lessons together. From the same dancing master they learned the figures of sarabande and minuet. They read together the song of Roland, the great hero of every French boy, and the stories of Arthur and his knights, and many another splendid old tale.

Everyone liked the merry, fair-haired girl.

" She's the most perfect child I've ever seen," said the king. And the queen added, " She has only to smile to turn any Frenchman's head! "

To show her regard for Scotland Mary sometimes put on a highland costume with the Stuart plaid. The courtiers declared her a goddess even in that astonishing garb.

" If she's so beautiful dressed like a savage," they asked, " what would she be in rich robes made *a la francaise?* "

No one could say enough about her sweetness and goodness as well as her beauty. Going home from church one Palm Sunday she looked so lovely as she walked along carrying the green palm branch that a woman in the crowd knelt down in the street and whispered, " Aren't you an angel? "

At the French court there was constant pleasure with a great many festivals in the parks and palaces. There were balls and picnics and hunting parties. There were various sports—falcon flying and hawking, tennis and archery. In that company of beautiful, clever ladies Mary Stuart, girl as she was, more than held her own. The king often spent an hour with her, " because," said he, "she talks as sensibly as a woman of twenty-five."

Very happily the time passed until Mary was sixteen, which was then considered a suitable age for marriage. "The wedding," the king announced, "shall be a dazzling scene. We'll spare neither pains nor expense!"

In the great cathedral of Notre Dame in Paris the marriage took place. The church was richly decorated. There were long lines of gorgeously dressed ladies and nobles, for the men wore almost as many jewels as the women.

More beautiful than ever Mary looked as she walked slowly up the aisle. Her wedding gown was white as a lily, embroidered with pearls. It had a long blue velvet train carried by two young girls. About her neck on a chain hung the "great Harry," a wonderful jewel that had belonged to her grandfather, Henry the seventh. The bride and groom walked to the doorway of the cathedral to put the ring on her finger, so that the immense crowds outside might see this part of the ceremony.

Afterwards there was a wedding supper followed by a splendid ball. The bride danced the minuet, stately and graceful. A gentleman bore her train which measured a full twelve yards. Before the festivities were over Mary was very tired. The great crown with all its precious stones seemed heavy. But to take it off would have been unlucky. So the king sent two lords to stand by her and hold it just over her head. For days the feasting and rejoicing went on with balls and masquerades and tournaments.

But across the Channel trouble was brewing. The queen of England, Mary Tudor, died. Her half-sister Elizabeth came to the throne. But the next heir was Mary Stuart, some people insisted, arguing that old Henry the eighth wasn't legally married to Elizabeth's mother. The new ruler of England ought to be not Elizabeth, but the queen of Scots.

When Mary Stuart appeared at the wedding of one of the dauphin's sisters the heralds called out, by the king's order, "All hail the queen of England! Make way, make way for the queen of Scotland and England!"

Now that was a very rash thing to do since it won for Mary no advantage whatsoever, but gave her a bitter enemy. News of it was promptly carried to Elizabeth in London. At once she began nursing thoughts of revenge.

Soon after this the French king died and the dauphin came to the throne. Mary was now sovereign of France as well as of Scotland. She and Francis were crowned in the cathedral at Rheims. But little they had to do with the actual government of the country.

The young king amused himself with hunting. The queen and her four Marys rode out to watch the sport or listened to the troubadours' songs or walked in the gardens by the winding Loire. Their little court of young people enjoyed itself thoroughly. But the health of Francis gradually failed. He was often sad and depressed.

Two great sorrows came to Mary—her mother's death, followed soon by her husband's. At seventeen she was orphan and widow. All in white she dressed, the royal mourning of those days. She was so lovely and attracted so much attention that people called her " the white queen."

The Scotch begged Mary to come back and rule over her native land. She remembered the cold, inhospitable climate and the stormy, dangerous journey. Shuddering she thought of Scotland as a place of exile. She decided to return, but with many regrets and misgivings. On the ship she went to the stern and knelt on the deck for hours, watching the French coast grow dim in the distance. She cried bitterly and said, " Farewell, oh France, and farewell! I shall never see thee more!"

In five days the boat reached Scotland. It was a very foggy afternoon, bleak and gray. It was muddy underfoot. Only a few people were on hand to welcome her. Staidly the sober Scots looked on while gallant young Frenchmen spread their cloaks in the mire where Mary must step.

Later there was a little celebration. But the trappings of the horses seemed poor and the lights meager in comparison with the splendor and luxury to which she was used. The poverty of the land was a sad contrast to sunny France. The bagpipes serenading at the gate of Holyrood, the gloomy old palace in Edinburgh, filled her with terror. A devout Catholic, she was dismayed when a group of Protestant reformers sang psalms under her windows.

But her youth and beauty and her sweet manners won the hearts of the common people. " A tall bit lassie to stand by Bruce's chair," said the men. " Heaven bless that sweet face! " added the women.

With skill and energy Mary Stuart took up her task of government, for she had real political ability. Five hours a day she gave to public affairs. Embroidering all the while in silk and gold, she listened to the advice of her councilors. Gravely she discussed matters of state with them.

Without delay she was for the second time beset with royal suitors. The kings of Sweden and Denmark asked her hand. The Spanish monarch proposed a marriage with his son. The holy Roman emperor offered his heir as her husband. Her brother-in-law in France wished to marry her. Elizabeth of England urged the Earl of Leicester, one of her favorite lords. But Mary took matters into her own hands. She chose her cousin Darnley.

She had almost made up her mind to accept him as a matter of wise policy. The marriage would combine their two claims to the throne of England. He was invited to visit at historic old Holyrood. When she saw that he was handsome and accomplished, easy and graceful in manner she loved him at once passionately. She determined to marry him though the plan was opposed by Elizabeth and by the Protestant party in Scotland and by many of the lords.

Unfortunately they were right and she was wrong. Happy for a time Mary lavished on Darnley every token of love, every mark of distinction. But he was a headstrong, inexperienced boy. His accomplishments were only showy. His fondness for music and poetry was a pose. He wasn't capable of returning a love such as hers.

Soon he became proud and haughty and selfish. His courtly manners and attractive face had veiled over his weak, vicious nature, but it showed through. Thoughtless he treated the queen with the greatest indifference. Once at a public banquet he spoke to her so rudely that she left the table in tears. Married in July, by Michaelmas Mary knew Darnley for a lovely husk of a man, empty of brain or heart.

Among the courtiers was an Italian, David Rizzio who was the queen's private secretary. He helped with her foreign correspondence. He could play the lute. He sang in a quartette. He wrote verses. Little by little his influence with Mary increased. She gave him many honors.

Darnley became jealous thinking Rizzio his rival. Some of the Scottish lords agreed with him saying, "This Italian's a low-born, foreign upstart. Though called a secretary, he's really minister." Together they plotted against him.

One windy night Mary and two of her ladies and Rizzio were having supper together. Darnley entered and sat down by the queen, the signal that everything was ready. Up the private stairs crept the leader of the conspirators. Boldly he walked into the room. His armor clanked on the floor.

"What's the meaning of this intrusion?" cried Mary alarmed and angry. "Begone, sir!"

The next moment torches gleamed in the passage. The little room was full of assassins.

"We mean you no harm," came their reply. "We only want the villain Davy who stands near you."

The servants rushed in to help the queen and Rizzio. The table was upset. The wretched secretary calling out "Save me, madame, save me!" was dragged from the room and across the hall to the head of the stairs. There Darnley and the nobles fell upon him all together, so wildly that they wounded one another in their fury.

The tattered body, stabbed no less than fifty-six times, was hurled to the foot of the steps. There Mary saw it with her husband's gold-hilted dagger still sticking in the breast. The picture never faded from her mind. That night the last of her love for Darnley died.

With her ladies-in-waiting the queen stood trembling and weeping. In a few minutes she dried her eyes.

"Farewell, tears," she said resolutely to herself, "I must study revenge."

Slowly she turned to her husband.

"Consider and remember well, my lord, what I now say. I shall never rest until I give you as sore a heart as I have at this hour."

Soon after this Mary's son was born. She named him James. The christening was a great festival with pageants and fireworks. Ambassadors from foreign lands came for the ceremony. Even Elizabeth as godmother sent a gift, a christening font of gold and enamel.

Now comes the great mystery in the life of this royal Mary. In the murder of Rizzio her weak husband was only a tool of the Scottish lords. One of them, the swaggering, brutal, brave Earl of Bothwell, now plotted against Darnley in turn. Gunpowder was placed under the house where he lay sick with the smallpox. There was an explosion. His lifeless body was found in the garden.

The Scots were astonished at these desperate crimes at the palace. But they were loyal to their queen. They would not believe her guilty.

Was Mary Stuart in this plot? I can't tell you. The books of history don't agree. Some of them say she knew the whole plan, that she went every day to see her husband just to throw people off the scent, and that she returned to Holyrood that Sunday night barely in time to escape being blown up herself.

" I must leave you," she said to Darnley with every show of affection. " You know the faithful Sebastien who came with me from France has married one of my maids. The servants are having a masque to celebrate the wedding. And I promised I'd be there before the evening's over, to dance at the feast. Good-night, my husband," and she kissed him.

Other writers argue that Mary knew nothing whatever of Bothwell's schemes. They insist, with many proofs for this opinion, that the famous " casket letters " which told the plot to kill Darnley were not in her handwriting at all, but were clever forgeries.

When the hawk-nosed, bearded earl was tried for this murder he rode to the court on one of Darnley's favorite horses, a present from the queen. From beginning to end the trial was a mere form. It lasted only a few hours. Bothwell was set free.

The Scots became suspicious. Openly they discussed Mary's share in the gunpowder affair. They denounced her shameless conduct. Instead of cheering there were murmurings and mutterings when she rode out with the earl. People spoke of them as " the red bridegroom and the pale bride." The disapproval of her subjects changed to indignation and horror when Mary Stuart set aside every thought except her own desire and married her husband's murderer.

This step lost her the loyal friendship of Scotland. Versed in politics was the queen. Through a maze of intrigue she could thread her way. But one thing she had never been taught— to keep her passions in check. With her love was an uncontrollable impulse. And now her love brought only tragedy to this Mary who had ruled all hearts.

For Bothwell, wild and reckless, was disliked by the people. The nobles hated him for his haughty, defiant manners. Promptly they rebelled and raised an army to protect the baby prince. It was a far larger force than the queen could summon though the gold christening font was melted down to pay her soldiers. She was of course defeated. Bothwell escaped to the continent. Just one month after her marriage day Mary was taken prisoner. The Scottish lords forced her to give up the throne to her son. In the same room at Stirling castle where she had been crowned the baby James was now proclaimed king.

Mary longed to escape from her island prison. Plan after plan was made but failed. Once the plot succeeded so far that she was actually seated in the boat when the whiteness and beauty of her hands betrayed her disguise. Finally with the help of a lad of fourteen she did escape, raised another army to fight against the regent, and was again defeated.

To whom could she turn?

" Seek protection in France," urged her friends.

But she determined to appeal to England. " Elizabeth sent me a ring," she said, " and promised her love and friendship. A woman, a cousin, a queen—there are three reasons for expecting aid."

But when she crossed the border Elizabeth refused to see her.

" She must first clear herself of the crimes with which the Scots have charged her."

Mary was neither welcome nor openly condemned. Instead the English waited for months and months and years, wearing out her heart with endless longing. It seemed as if they wanted to avoid the responsibility and let time and grief and anguish cause her death. To all her pleas the haughty Elizabeth turned a deaf ear. Again and again she refused an audience. Did she remember Mary Stuart heralded in France as ruler of England?

A guest in name but really a prisoner, the fugitive queen was moved about from one English castle to another. With each move she was more closely confined. More of her good friends were banished from her side. She entered her first prison a beautiful woman of twenty-five. She left the last still beautiful, but broken and faded with snow-white hair.

All those twenty years she was the center of innumerable plots. Scotch and English Catholics, the pope, Spain and France and Austria were scheming to secure her freedom. They wanted to dethrone Elizabeth and make England and Scotland Catholic again. Constantly Mary Stuart plotted with them, for busy scheming was her joy. She had an ambition for power that nothing could satisfy.

" Yes," she confessed openly, " I sympathize with all the plans made for my escape. But," she always added, " I deny that I am aiding any plot against my cousin's life."

Elizabeth urged, perhaps with truth, " England and the English church will never be safe while Mary lives."

She asked Parliament to pass a law that conspirators and those for whom they were plotting should alike suffer death. Finally one project more dangerous than most was discovered. Mary was brought to trial in an English court.

Though she had no lawyer and no papers for days she held in check forty of the ablest men of England, thanks to her wit and presence of mind. As you can guess she was found guilty of being concerned in this plot. The judges had been told what to say. After long delay Elizabeth signed the warrant

SHE ENTERED HER FIRST PRISON A BEAUTIFUL WOMAN OF TWENTY-FIVE

for her death. Her son, a king on his throne, raised not a hand to help her.

Solemnly the English commissioners read the warrant to Mary.

"When?" she asked.

"Sentence will be carried out to-morrow morning at eight o'clock."

Most of the night she spent writing her will, remembering all her friends. Calmly she prepared for the beheading.

"Dress me," she told her maids, "as for a festival, in the robes of a queen."

They chose a gown of black velvet with the train embroidered in gold. Over her head she put a long, white crêpe veil, about her neck a rosary and golden crucifix. With two of her Marys she entered the great hall.

She saw the scaffold and the block, covered with black velvet. She saw the gleaming ax and the executioner in black, with a band of red crêpe on his arm. Unafraid Mary Stuart faced the world and death.

"Bear witness," she said, turning to one of her friends, "that I die firm in my religion, a true Scotchwoman and true to France. Commend me to my dearest and most sweet son. Tell him if he will live in the fear of God I doubt not he shall do well. He shall have the blessing of God in heaven as I now give him mine on earth."

Taking the crucifix in her hands Mary knelt down and prayed for herself and for Elizabeth. Then the executioner first asking her pardon on his knees, did his work. He held up her beautiful head exclaiming, " So perish all the enemies of the Queen!"

The spectators were in tears. Only one of them could give the answer, " Amen." For Mary's queenly bearing and her sad story made them all feel a sense of shame at the manner of her death.

The most charming princess of her time, Mary Stuart was also the most unhappy. Very beautiful and winning, she was a queen to live and die for. And many died.

Years later her ambitious dreams came true. Her son James lived in London, king of England and Scotland. The body of his mother he moved to Westminster Abbey where you can see it now, near the tomb of the cousin Elizabeth whom she never saw.

ON PLYMOUTH ROCK

Mary Chilton Winslow: c. 1606–1679

"WHY, why," Mary looked about her with a perplexed face, "why, we're going back! Can that be right? Surely England was on the other side of the ship yesterday. What's happened? Is the *Speedwell* going back too?"

She ran to the rail and gazed at the *Mayflower's* convoy. Yes, there she was with her sails spread, following not very far behind.

"Tell me, Mother, what's wrong?" Mary Chilton said when she made her way back across the slippery deck to her mother's side. "I'm almost grown up. You must let me take Isabella's place. Tell me, why does Master Bradford look so anxious as he talks there with Father?"

"Your father has not told me much, child. The *Speedwell* is leaking. Her captain says she'll never stand the trip to Virginia. Her freight and her passengers must be put on our vessel."

27

Mary's eyes grew brighter and her cheeks flushed as the thought came to her mind, " The Winslows are on the *Speedwell* and now ——"

She turned suddenly to her mother.

" But where in the world will we put them all? We're already crowded—in the men's quarters and where we womenfolk are stowed away. Packed in like fish in a keg, I heard Captain Jones saying to the mate. Twice as many as the *Mayflower* was planned to carry. What can we do with more goods and more people? "

" I don't know, child," answered Mistress Susanna Chilton. "Governor Carver and Master Bradford will decide. The voyage is delayed again. That's why the men look anxious. They wanted to arrive by the end of September and now ——"

" Oh, Mother, what a journey it's been, just one delay after another! The slow trip on the canal-boat from Leyden to Delfthaven, and saying good-bye to sister Isabella and her husband; and crossing to Southampton and days and days there for loading; and no sooner started than the *Speedwell* began to leak and we turned back to Dartmouth and waited eleven days to patch and mend her. And now, only three days later, before we're out of sight of England, the same story over again! "

Back to Plymouth sailed the two ships and nine precious days were lost while colonists and sailors unloaded the *Speedwell's* cargo and made a place for barrels and boxes and crates in the hold of the *Mayflower*. But make room for her twenty,

passengers they could not. Only a dozen could be accommo-
dated.

Master Edward Winslow was one of these, and his brother
Gilbert. But the younger brother John, they decided, should
stay in England. Mary Chilton said not a word to anyone.
But—how disappointed she was! It was far worse than having
him on the other ship!

At last on the sixth of September they were off.

" Our third start," Mary said to Remember Allerton; " let's
hope it'll be the charm! "

What a voyage that was! They left Plymouth in a fine gale
and met the full force of the equinoctial storms. When the
green waves were at their highest they flung themselves wildly
at the *Mayflower,* tossing her this way and that as if she were
a cockle-shell. Mist and fog were so dense the captain could
not see the sun and lost his reckoning completely. They were
carried out of their course, far to the north of the mouth of
Hudson River.

The winds were so fierce, the seas so high that at times they
sped along without a bit of sail up, drifting under bare poles.
Wave after wave swept across the decks and the water leaked
through until Desire Minter would say, " Mary, is this the
Speedwell we're sailing on? "

In the women's cabins it was close and uncomfortable.
Everywhere there was overcrowding. A hundred and two
people, and a crew of thirty, on that little vessel, only a hundred feet long. It was wet. It was cold. The only place for

cooking was over the boxes of earth the women took out on deck in calm weather. The rest of the time, day after day, week after week, they ate dried meat, hard ship's bread and cheese.

One afternoon Mary and Elizabeth Tilley heard the alarm, "Man overboard!" John Alden, the cooper, cried out that John Howland had been swept across the deck and thrown headlong into the sea.

"Head the ship into the wind," the captain shouted to the man at the wheel.

With a boat-hook he fished young Howland out of the water. The girls saw him sprawling on the deck, still holding on to the halyard that he had seized as he went overboard. Elizabeth's face was very white. Mary teased her about John. Did they guess that one day she would be his wife?

Captain Jones told the Pilgrim leaders that they must return to England. In the storm a deck-beam had cracked and bent. At any moment it might give way. There was no possible means of mending it, there on the ocean, or in the wilderness if it held till they reached Virginia. Best go back at once to an English shipyard.

One of the colonists was a carpenter from Leyden. He had a great jack-screw among his tools. Why not, he proposed, force the broken beam back into place and prop it up with a couple of stout timbers? This was done and in some of the pictures you can see those props.

And another day, the most important of the voyage, though

no one knew it at the time, the forty-one men gathered in the main cabin. On the lid of Captain Standish's chest they signed a compact to regulate their civil government in the new world. Women and girls had no share in this business, which proved to be the first step in a government of and by and for the people.

After the storms came milder, warmer days. This was when Mistress Hopkins' baby was born, a fine boy. Mary Chilton exclaimed to the other girls, " What a splendid name to choose for him—Oceanus! "

On the tenth of November the longed-for cry, " Land ho! " rang out at daybreak. Mary dressed quickly and hurried up on deck.

" The end of our voyage," she was saying to herself. " Land! "

There it was—a line of white rising above the gray-blue of the sea, a low-lying coast with sandy beach, a bold headland, and hills covered with dense woods. The place? To-day it is called Provincetown. She could hear the low, muffled roar of the surf. The ship was anchored fully three-quarters of a mile offshore. She heard the second mate Coppin say something about shallow water.

Well, this was the end of their voyage. Now their troubles were over. Her father had not been well during these last days. He'd be all right again as soon as they were on land.

But Mary Chilton was wrong in thinking troubles had ended.

Perhaps they'd only begun? She was not to see the last of the crowded *Mayflower,* not for many a long day, not for many weeks. How impatient she was to go ashore immediately! How she laughed at herself when her mother asked, " Where would you sleep? What would you eat? And what about the Indians, Mary? "

She watched the longboat taking the first party of men ashore, saw them run aground, saw them leap overboard into surf knee-high, waist-high when the waves struck them. Oh, how cold the water looked! Yes, she'd be glad to stay on the ship a little longer!

A couple of mornings later Mary climbed down the swaying rope ladder into the longboat. Someone tossed down her big roll of linen. Her mother must stay with her father, she must go with the women to do the two months' laundry. What a day's work it was—washing in the fresh water of the beach pond, hanging things on the bushes to dry, eating a bit of cold lunch, while the men stood guard in case the savages came into sight!

Stormy days followed and cold. Only at high tide could the boat take a party ashore for wood and water. Every man who made the trip caught cold from wading in the surf, and coughed and coughed. There the Pilgrims were, anchored in the harbor, with no hopes of living on land for the present. And many sick there were, Master James Chilton among them, suffering from colds and coughs and fever. Good Dr. Fuller went from one to another, stopping in the women's cabins to see the babies—Oceanus, and Peregrine White, born there at Provincetown.

There was constant talk of a site for the colony. It must have a deep harbor, fresh water, cleared land so that crops could be planted early in the spring, and a hill for easier defense against the Indians. One, two, three exploring trips were made to search for such a place, with Miles Standish in command.

On the *Mayflower* scarcely one person was free from cold and cough, and some were very ill indeed. Mistress Chilton nursed her husband faithfully and did all she could to make him comfortable. He grew worse and worse. Hope of his getting better faded in her heart.

" Oh, Mary," the poor woman would say, " oh, daughter, what will become of us if he is taken? Yet—God's will be done."

A week before Christmas, on a gloomy day with a strong gale blowing and rain that turned to snow by night, James Chilton died. This was the third death among the passengers, the first head of a family. Poor Mary! The next morning, after the men had fetched a supply of drinking water and Juniper wood, they held a service for her father and the burying party was sent ashore.

When the explorers returned Mary could take little interest in the Indian corn they brought, or in the baskets and pottery they found in a big mound. She wasn't excited over Patience Brewster's news that the site was found at last. Still she was glad when they weighed anchor, after five weeks in that harbor, and sailed away to Plymouth.

"Why do they call it Plymouth?" she asked. "Is it, Priscilla, because we came from Plymouth?"

"No, though that might be a reason. John Alden says the map Captain John Smith made has this place marked 'Plimoth.' It was named by the king's son."

A mile or more from land they anchored in the new harbor. When the working party started ashore there was no longer the problem of landing in shallow water and getting wet through in the surf. The men had found a great boulder shelving from the shore into the sea. The longboat could come right up to it, the first mate pointed out, and they could step off in comfort. The "landing rock" they called it, that great piece of granite that was, like the Pilgrims themselves, a wanderer, dropped in that spot by some arctic glacier. It was the threshold into Plymouth colony, the gateway of a nation.

Christmas day? No celebration at all, not even for the children. Christmas was not kept by the Pilgrims. They were opposed to all saints' days. So for that first twenty-fifth of December the record boasts not of a celebration, but of the work accomplished. A large party went ashore to fell trees and begin the building of the common-house.

A church service in this house was announced for the third Sunday in January. The thatched roof wasn't finished, but the walls were far enough along. In England the Pilgrims had often held their service under the sky.

SHE WAS THE FIRST WOMAN TO LAND AT PLYMOUTH

So the longboat brought ashore, for the second time in the new world, a group of women. The children crowded forward eagerly as they neared the landing rock. The sailors made ready. In the bow stood Mary Chilton. The boat touched the rock. She poised herself a second and sprang out, reaching up to the outstretched hands of the nearest man to steady her footing on the wet stone. The wind and spray had dashed some color into her pale cheeks. She was excited at being the first woman to land at Plymouth!

But that fact was not important enough for Captain Jones to mention in the *Mayflower's* log, or for Master Bradford to include in his history of Plymouth. The story of her being first to land, or at least the first woman to step on Plymouth rock was passed down by word of mouth, merely a tradition, until her granddaughter put it into writing in 1773.

Worse and worse grew the epidemic of sickness. At one time there were only six well persons to care for all the others. In February at its height two, and sometimes three died in a day. Mary Chilton's mother died, and Elizabeth Tilley's, and Priscilla's. Master White, the baby's father, died; and the governor's wife, and the doctor's assistant. Mistress Allerton died, and Captain Standish's pretty, frail wife; and others till only half the Pilgrims were left.

At night when no lurking Indians might see, the bodies were carried up to the hill overlooking the harbor, wrapped in canvas, and buried there. The ground was carefully leveled so that it would give no count of the deaths. In the spring corn was planted over the graves. For those who loved them, there was not even the comfort of seeing stones marked with their names. But as long as mayflowers blossom in Plymouth town, their memory will live.

In January the Pilgrims had portioned off the land for their homes. The unmarried men and the orphaned children were divided among the others, so that there were nineteen families in all. But when the common-house was finished, so many had died that only seven houses were needed. Mary Chilton lived with the Brewsters.

Wistfully her eyes followed the *Mayflower* when she set sail for England early in April. Like the others she had said "No," when Captain Jones offered to take back with him any who wished to go—free of charge if the women would nurse the sick among his crew. There was a parting salute from the ship. Captain Standish's guns boomed out their answer. Mary Chilton, the only member of her family, was alone in Plymouth.

Her days were full of tasks. She helped Mistress Brewster with the housework. She looked after the children. She washed with Constance Hopkins at the brook. She helped prepare herbs and witch-hazel, for Dr. Fuller's supply of medicines must not get too low.

One November day she was busy at this work when Elizabeth Tilley rushed in, all excited.

"Oh, Mary, a ship's coming into the harbor! No, not the *Mayflower,* it's too small. Do come and see!"

Mistress Brewster nodded permission and off the girls ran. Nearer and nearer came the ship. Was it English? Yes, at last they could see the flag. Elizabeth was right, it was smaller than the *Mayflower*, than the *Speedwell* even. Just before the anchor was dropped they made out her name: the *Fortune*.

All the colonists gathered to watch the longboat come ashore. Gilbert Winslow pushed through the crowd as his brother John stepped out on the landing rock, and seized him by the shoulders. How Mary's heart beat! How hot her face felt! But in the excited crowd, for no one had known of the *Fortune's* coming, she passed unnoticed. John Winslow had come to Plymouth—at last!

The records do not tell us just when these two were married, save that it was before 1627. Indeed the only reason why Mary Chilton's name is mentioned was because her brother-in-law, Edward Winslow, was three times governor of the colony.

If you've been feeling sorry for Mary, you needn't any longer. Her troubles were over. She began to be very happy in Plymouth. Her husband's affairs went well. The colony grew. Because of religious persecutions in England thousands came to the new world. Plymouth was overcrowded. There was not enough pasturage for their cattle. Settlers moved to Marshfield and across the harbor to Duxbury.

With this influx of colonists enterprising John Winslow began buying land and trading in real estate. A successful business he made of it. He moved his family up to Boston; that was more convenient for his work, and so many of their old friends had left Plymouth that Mary was glad to go.

In Boston too they prospered. John Winslow became a merchant, trading to the West Indies in his own vessels. A fine home they had, near the Old South Church, at what is to-day the corner of Devonshire Street and Spring Lane. Next door lived Governor Winthrop.

Ten children came to John and Mary Chilton Winslow. And along with that big family came prosperity that enabled them to live with ease and comfort. What a contrast to that first year at Plymouth! How his business had grown is shown by John Winslow's will: his bark *Mary* and his ketch *Speedwell,* with cargoes of pork and sugar and tobacco, were to be divided among the children. The Boston house, with land and gardens and a goodly sum of money, was to be his wife's. The whole estate came to just under three thousand pounds.

In the probate registry in Boston you can see to-day the will of Mary Chilton Winslow. The only others made by *May-flower* passengers which are still in existence, are the wills of Miles Standish and of William Mullins, Priscilla's father. What luxuries this Mary had! Silver spoons and pewter dishes, rugs, silk gowns and petticoats valued at six pounds, ten shillings, seventeen linen caps and fourteen headbands, six white aprons, napkins worth seven shillings—all these she gives away. To each of her children, a silver cup with a handle. To one daughter, her best gown and petticoat and her silver bowl; to a grandson a great silver tankard; to a granddaughter a trunk of linen, with a bed and bolsters; to another her pretty coat with silver lace. In the crowded quarters of the *Mayflower* did she ever dream of owning such articles? At the end of the will, the signature—not her name, but her mark M, very neatly made.

In the front of King's Chapel Burying-ground in Boston, beneath the Winslow coat of arms, she was buried. To-day through the iron palings you can see the slab from the Tremont Street side. In old Plymouth town Chilton Street shows that the colonists remembered the eager girl who was the first woman to step on the landing rock. And the famous rock you see there also, marked with the simple inscription " 1620."

It was the threshold of a new world, for Mary Chilton and for all the Pilgrims—a world where they would have freedom of worship according to men's consciences, not according to a king's decree; a world whose conquest is a story of hardships, of trials and tribulations, of pestilence and death; to meet and overcome them unflinching faith and persistence and fortitude were needed—and these the Pilgrim women had, as well as their men.

Honor then to all of them, and perhaps most of all to Mary, Chilton!

THE "ROSE OF EPPING FOREST"

Mary Ball Washington: 1708–1789

"WHOA, WHOA!" cried the driver of the chaise. "Whoa there! Something's wrong!"

Before he could stop the horses the chaise was upset. The man scrambled out from the tangle of harness and splintered wood and broken glass. His first thought was for the safety of his passenger. This rich American planter traveling through the south of England would not relish delays and fractured bones.

His passenger proved to be injured, seriously injured. The driver ran to summon aid. People came to help carry the stranger to the nearest house.

Slowly the handsome man in the ruined chaise regained his health. He had plenty of time to study the pretty young woman who helped to nurse him. How attractive she looked whenever she came into the room! Her hair was like flax. Her

He Could Picture Her Paying Morning Calls in Her Sedan Chair

cheeks were like mayblossoms. Good friends the two became during the long weeks of his convalescence, even though he was fourteen years older.

How surprised he was to learn that she wasn't English at all, but American like himself! She lived in Virginia in the very county adjoining his estate on the Potomac. She was only visiting some relatives there in Berkshire.

Winsome and demure was Mary Ball, sensible and modest. Little by little Augustine Washington recalled things he'd heard about her. The people at home called her " the Rose of Epping Forest," from the name of Joseph Ball's plantation— a pretty title it was with a touch of real Virginia gallantry, " the Rose of Epping Forest."

At the dances in Williamsburg, the gay capital of the colony, she was a great belle and won many a social triumph. He could picture her bowing in the stately minuet, paying morning calls in her sedan chair, driving in a heavy coach drawn by four horses. He remembered tales of her beauty—indeed they weren't exaggerated—and of her lovers who toasted her gallantry in the high-flown, complimentary language of that day.

Why had she never married? Most girls did in Virginia, at sweet sixteen or before. And now she was two and twenty. Was she hard to please? Or was it merely that she was calm and self-controlled? Well, she'd had a long and happy girlhood. That showed in her face. He smiled as another bit of gossip flashed across his mind—how after some months in society she had settled down as a schoolgirl again and studied with her little sister when some lucky chance brought into their neighborhood a teacher educated at Oxford.

"And if her schooling is a matter of shreds and patches as she laughingly says," thought the invalid, "she knows all about keeping house—not in London, but in the wilds of America as Englishmen call Virginia. Epping Forest's a big plantation. And the Balls are important people too. Why, they left Britain and went to the Old Dominion some years before our family did. They were landed gentry with a coat of arms and a Latin motto on their crest. And they've nearly as much English history back of them as the Washingtons!

"Ball and Washington—were the names joined once before? Ah, yes, I remember now. During Bacon's rebellion the loyal forces were led by two colonels—a Washington and a Ball. History repeats itself, they say. But—when all's said and done, a housekeeper, a homemaker's what a widower and his two little boys need."

From friendship these two Virginians meeting by chance in the south of England soon became lovers. Before long they were married.

Is all this a true story?

Perhaps. Tradition says so and even points out the pretty English cottage where they lived for a brief time in 1730. It's a charming and attractive legend, don't you think? Less prosaic than a plain, every-day tale of neighborhood friendship that blossomed into a middle-aged widower's marriage.

Whether Mary Ball ever visited her English relatives or

not, whether Augustine Washington went to London on a business trip or not, we can't be sure. The truth is these two had ample opportunity to meet right at home. Washington was a near neighbor of Major George Eskridge, near as they counted in that day when Virginia plantations were large and distances were great. Fifteen or twenty miles apart, a mere nothing of travel, were Sandy Point and Wakefield. Why didn't this widower meet the pretty, young "Rose of Epping Forest" at the Eskridge house since the major was her guardian? And only a mile and a half away from Sandy Point lived her married sister Elizabeth.

Well, be the story of the chaise true or merely a tradition, the histories of Virginia report that soon after their marriage they were settled at Wakefield, the old Washington homestead on Bridge's creek. A mile wide, the thousand acres of wood and fertile bottom land sloped down to the Potomac River. The house to which the bride came was large and old-fashioned, with low-stretching roof and dormer windows. And here in February, 1732, was born their son George, the image of his mother Mary.

Now it was the custom in Virginia to name the first boy after his father or grandfather. But Mary Ball had too much strength of mind to follow custom blindly. Her son was christened for the " trusty and well-beloved George Eskridge," as the mother's will described him. What greater tribute could Mary Ball, left to his care at twelve years old, pay to his faithful guardianship?

There were other children too—Betty and Samuel, named for the married sister and her husband; and later three more, born at the Ferry Farm to which they moved when Wakefield burned.

That disaster came on a windy April day when Mr. Washington was away from home. The men were firing a brush heap in the garden. Some sparks were carried to the roof. The house was in flames before anyone discovered it. There was no hope of saving it with the river four hundred yards away.

Instead of lamenting and wringing her hands Mary Washington showed a calm self-control. She set an example to the excited group of slaves and children. She began carrying out furniture and clothing. She took valuables to a safe place. She gave orders like a general. In the emergency she could plan quickly.

" Prepare supper," she said to the servants, " and put up the beds in the little cabin you've been using as a kitchen." And there they supped in great content.

The house was never rebuilt. To-day its site is marked by a solitary chimney and a small, engraved stone.

For their new home Augustine Washington chose a spot on the bank of the Rappahannock opposite the town of Fredericksburg. Like the other it was a broad, low house with four large rooms and a spacious attic. They called it Pine Grove from the noble body of trees that grew near it. But their friends and neighbors always called it the Ferry Farm.

Thirteen years after their marriage Augustine Washington died. Courageously his wife took up her difficult duties. The will made her guardian of the children and of all their property, but with this condition—that she remain unmarried. Remember that she was a second wife—isn't that amusing?

What a burden all this business was! Each son inherited a plantation—more than five thousand acres in all, scattered through four Virginia counties. There were notes and shares in iron works for Betty. But this property gave their mother little ready money. And she had five small children to educate.

Mary Washington was young—only thirty-five—and handsome. She was mistress of a fine estate. She was closely connected by ties of marriage and friendship with all the important families of that neighborhood. She could have chosen a gay life of pleasures, a round of enjoyments. She could have been a leader in Virginia society. She chose the better part—what Goethe says marks the most excellent woman—to be as a father to her children.

She was not only their loving mother. She was guardian and adviser, responsible for their upbringing and their business affairs. "Keep your land and it will keep you," said the old adage. The plantations must not only be kept intact, they must provide an income for daily expenses and a margin for education. Wisely she planned for her sons to earn their own living.

Her stepsons had been sent to school in England. For George this was an impossible expense. She gave him the best training available—first in a school taught by the parish sexton, then in one farther away so that he rode ten miles and back each day, and later at the old academy in Fredericksburg. Here he laid the foundation of his education.

But it was his mother who cast mind and heart in the right mould. It was she who taught him a love of order and method, who showed him the value of time, who made him realize that if a thing was worth doing at all, it was worth doing well and exactly. It was from her he learned courage to bear great responsibilities. It was from her he learned the strict obedience which must precede the power to command.

After 1743 Mary Washington had two absorbing interests— the care of a thriving plantation, the training of her children. A plain, comfortable home she gave them, marked by abundance but never by extravagance or waste. Very strictly she brought them up. Silently they listened to the talk of older people. They spoke when spoken to. To the unquestioning obedience of soldiers they were trained. She passed on to them habits of industry, economy, usefulness. Most important of all, on each child she impressed the beautiful, religious faith that was hers. To do justly, to love mercy, to walk humbly with God—this she taught them by lesson and example.

Never idle for a moment herself, Mary Washington was a stern mistress. She talked little, but her words had clearness and force. There was a plain truth and honesty about her. For all her kindness and her cheerfulness she awed the children's friends.

" It's because she's so stately and dignified," one of them explained.

And another commented, " If she came into the room we were all as mute as mice."

" Why," one of the cousins said, " I was more afraid of Madam Washington than of my own parents! "

Grave respect and compliance with her commands she required of them as children. They gave her both to the end of her life. " Honored Madam," their letters would begin; and more than one of them still in existence is signed " Your obedient son," when that son had become the most illustrious of Americans.

In many, many details you can see the imprint of her sterling character stamped on George Washington. It was her teaching, her discipline, her precepts that were the basis of his fortune and his fame.

" All that I am," he often said, " I owe to my mother."

What we are as a nation we owe to him. His debt to Mary Ball Washington, many times multiplied, is ours.

Wise mother as she was, she was as wise a business woman. She herself kept the accounts for the different plantations. She supervised all the work in the fields—a complicated and difficult task in any place, and especially so in Virginia where all the crops were raised with slave labor.

" And negroes," she used to say, " are no better than grown-up children. They have to be told and watched constantly."

For each estate she had an overseer to whom she gave directions. The most exact obedience she demanded. Once after she had given certain orders she took the manager to task for not following them to the letter.

"But in my judgment, madam," he began explaining his action. He intended to add that the result was better than if he'd carried out her instructions. But he had no chance to defend himself.

"Who gave you the right," she interrupted, "to use your judgment in this matter? I command, sir. There's nothing left for you but to obey!"

"Her eyes flashed blue lightning," the man said when he told the story afterwards. "I felt as if I'd been knocked down."

It was her custom always to inspect for herself. She made the rounds of the different plantations. With keen eyes for any disorder or neglect she looked at fields and gardens, at the negro quarters, at barns and fences. She kept the most careful records. As each son came of age she turned over his property to him worth far more than at the time of the father's death, for she was a thrifty housewife and a wise manager.

But outdoor supervision was only a part of her work. After the cotton was gathered and the seeds laboriously picked out by hand, it must be spun and woven. The wool from their sheep must be washed and carded and made into homespun. The spinning wheels which to-day you see only in museums whirled and buzzed at the Ferry Farm. Mary Washington herself cut out the garments for all the slaves on the estate and taught the women to sew.

All supplies she kept under lock and key. She weighed out sugar and flour, she measured molasses and vinegar to be used in the kitchen or at the negro quarters. She went bustling about with an enormous bunch of keys, so big a bunch that she carried it around in a wicker key-basket lined with leather. On Sundays too? No, then the basket was safely locked away in a closet. Off she went to church with the closet key hanging from her belt alongside a pincushion and scissors. What quaint pictures of this Mary have come down to us!

You must remember that long ago every plantation had to depend upon itself. There were no stores nearer than Williamsburg or Annapolis. Housekeepers couldn't buy any canned goods. Imagine the labor of preserving and pickling and drying vegetables and fruits, of curing bacon and ham by the hundred pounds! All this work Mary Washington superintended. Her household was famous for its order and economy. It ran so exactly that neighbors used to set their watches by the ringing of her bells.

"Sir," said her son years later when a guest arrived tardily for a state dinner, "I have a cook who never asks whether the company has come, but whether the hour has come."

Besides all this Mary Washington was doctor and druggist and nurse for her own family and for all the negroes too. She knew cunning secrets of herbs and leaves. She prepared balsams and lotions. Every dose of medicine she gave with her own hands. Often she watched all night, or night after night with a sick slave.

The marriage of her stepson Lawrence to pretty Mistress Anne Fairfax brought changes in the family life. At Mount Vernon, his fine estate on the Potomac, English and colonial officers were constant guests. Mary Washington sensed that meeting such men should be a part of her son's education, so she let George pay long visits there.

In the lad the martial spirit was strong. He listened to talk of wars and battles. He heard prophecies of more fighting— with the Indians, with the French—before a lasting peace could come to the colonies. After each visit he went home eagerly begging his mother to let him go to sea, for most of the guests at Mount Vernon were, like their host, in the British navy.

A request from Lawrence brought the boy a midshipman's appointment in the English squadron. They prepared his outfit, George gaily, his mother sadly. The man-of-war was anchored in the Potomac. Even his luggage had been taken aboard. He was, the story goes, already dressed in his middy's uniform. But Mary Washington hesitated.

Well she knew the danger to health, the temptations to the untried lad that the new life threatened. What reason was there for his being thrown on the world at fourteen, separated from his people? This would take him away permanently. What future did the navy offer a midshipman?

None whatever, if he has no money or influence, her brother

in England had written in answer to this question. Better make him a tinker's apprentice! So difficult is it for a man ever to get as high as to be master of a Virginia ship!

With such arguments as these Mary Washington talked with her son. She refused to let him go. The boy persisted. She changed to pleading. When George saw her rare tears he gave up his plan. Tragic it must have seemed at the time. But she was his mother, therefore she was right.

" Once more," he said to her when years later they recalled this incident, " once more I thank you for preventing a step that would have been fatal to my future."

If he could not have his heart's desire, she would give him every possible advantage at home. What was his favorite study? Mathematics. A special tutor was engaged. George learned surveying and through the Fairfax influence was appointed public surveyor of the county. This made it necessary for him to live with his brother at Mount Vernon. But often he visited his mother at Pine Grove and advised her about the management of her property.

When young George Washington was chosen by the governor of Virginia to carry the fatal dispatches to the French on the Ohio, he stopped to see his mother on his way to Williamsburg. He explained his errand. Immediately she saw all the perils of that journey.

" Oh, this fighting and killing! " she exclaimed and entreated him not to go. He convinced her that it was his duty to his country. At once she became calm. Laying her hand upon his shoulder she said solemnly, " Remember, God is our sure trust. To Him I commend you."

After his triumphant return he was invited to serve on Braddock's staff. A tempting offer for a young Virginia colonel, surely. Straight down to Mount Vernon drove Mary Washington when she heard this news.

" I beg you," she urged her son, " not to risk a life so dear to me and so valuable to the country. A dashing Irishman is this Braddock, reckless and brave. Can't some other officer be found to take your place? "

" I must go," came his reply. " I have no choice. I've been selected for this work. The country needs me."

For two days they discussed the matter. Between mother and son there was the fullest sympathy, the greatest affection. But he was now a man and must decide for himself. She could no longer dictate. His last argument she could not answer.

" The God to whom you commended me, Madam, when I set out on a more dangerous errand, defended me from all harm. And I trust He'll do so now. Don't you? "

Back at Pine Grove Mary Washington heard of the plans for the expedition and its starting west. Then word came of the ambush and of Braddock's defeat, of the death of more than sixty officers. Among the number was her son's name. Not for a fortnight did his letter arrive telling of his miraculous escape, of the four bullets that passed through his coat and the two horses shot under him. No wonder the Indians said he bore a charmed life!

What a story there was to tell when he finally reached Mount Vernon—of the illness which had forced him to ride in a wagon for ten days; of the splendid picture made by red coats and gold lace and flashing arms against the background of the somber forest; of the trap into which the army marched in spite of warnings of savage warfare; of how the British shouted " God save the king! " and fired at the hidden enemy and were themselves shot down in the open; of how they fled in wild retreat and only the Virginians saved the day from absolute disaster.

" You'd better have stayed at home," commented his mother grimly as she nursed him back to health, " and cultivated your farm."

During his five years of service in the French and Indian war she was very anxious about him. Young as he was he was commander-in-chief of Virginia's forces. Three hundred and fifty miles of frontier he must protect from savage raids. His men had no equipment, scanty provisions, sometimes not even shoes. Crazed with fear the settlers fled to Washington for help. The women's tears touched his heart so that he declared he'd offer his own life if that could save the people.

At last the fall of Quebec announced the end of French rule in America. He could leave the army and live quietly at Mount Vernon, a country gentleman. " There was no end to my trouble while George was in the army," the mother said with a feeling of relief, " but he has now given it up."

There followed for Mary Washington years of peaceful

home life. It was the high tide of prosperity in Virginia. Her business affairs were thriving. Betty married the young and handsome colonel, Fielding Lewis, and lived near by in Fredericksburg. Her brother George gave her away and all the guests remarked how much alike they were. Indeed they both resembled their mother in form and carriage and shape of face.

With great pride all the family heard of George's election to the house of burgesses and of his first appearance there, when the speaker thanked him for his services to Virginia and added as he was too confused to reply, " Sit down, Mr. Washington. Your modesty equals your valor."

Early in 1759 came another occasion for rejoicing. There was a brilliant wedding at the little church—her eldest son, the tall bridegroom in blue and scarlet uniform, riding away beside the coach and six that bore the radiant, little bride. Theirs had been a brief engagement.

" The truth is," explained Martha Custis shyly to her girl friends, " my estate's getting in a bad way and I need a man to look after it."

Mary Washington was exultant. Now her son was safe. His wife was beautiful and very rich. All the fighting and killing, all the danger of frontier journeys and of war were over and done with. They'd settle down at Mount Vernon. She could enjoy a serene and happy old age. The other children married—Samuel no less than five times—and lived near her. Grandchildren were growing up about her. More than once, in the traditional gown of black brocade, she stood godmother for girls and boys in Betty's family, in Samuel's, in John's.

But far in the north came a little cloud no larger than a man's hand.

She was alone now at Pine Grove. Her life was filled with interests and occupation. Her hands were always busy—with knitting, sewing, sorting fleeces for Virginia cloth, preserving fruits, distilling herbs and medicines for the sick. Never rich herself, she was so industrious and economical that she was able to give generously to the poor. A serene old age, she had promised herself.

England passed the stamp act and the first resistance to this measure came in Virginia. Then it was repealed. Men thought the little cloud had vanished. There followed the difficulty over tea. The colonies answered by refusing to import anything from the mother country. The port of Boston was ordered closed and Virginia observed a day of solemn fasting when this was put into effect.

Like her eldest son Mary Washington thought at first that war should be avoided. She was a loyal subject of the king, a devoted churchwoman. She was bound to England and the English church by many ties—early prejudices, traditions, ideas of duty, kindred. When war was declared she gave vent to her anguish.

"Oh, is there to be more fighting, more bloodshed? Surely it will all end in the halter!"

So bitter were her feelings that when her son rode over to

Fredericksburg to urge her to move to a place of safety, he was doubtful how she would receive him. It was prudent to stop at a little inn and reconnoiter. No one dared tell his mother. But she noticed the air of mystery in the servants' faces and demanded the reason.

"Tell George to come home instantly—instantly!" she ordered.

He was summoned to Boston to take command of the army, he told her. He begged her to move down to Mount Vernon. The storm was at hand. Betty offered her home in Fredericksburg. But Mary Washington refused.

"I've been a widow for more than thirty years. I'm used to my own way of living. I like my own house and my own servants. I'm no visitor. My days are busy and full, for the plantation can't get on without me. I will stay."

They continued to urge the dangers, to which she replied, "I thank you, children, for your affectionate and dutiful offers. But my wants are few. I'm perfectly competent to take care of myself." And to Fielding Lewis when he insisted on taking over the farm work she said, "Well, then, do you keep my books in order, for your eyesight's better than mine. But leave the managing to me."

At length she yielded to George's repeated arguments and chose a house in Fredericksburg. It was smaller and plainer than Pine Grove; she said it suited her simple style of living. Busy as he was before starting north, with public and private affairs, her son superintended her moving. Flowers and box were transplanted to make the new garden like her old one.

Always in pleasant weather in her two-wheeled chaise or in the little phaeton George sent her, she drove down to the ferry and aboard the boat. Once across the river she made the rounds of the farm. She inspected the growing crops. She ordered repairs and bought supplies. All the details she watched as carefully as in the years when she was managing her children's property.

Every night she walked out to the stables to watch the cows milked and the horses bedded down. Even then her busy fingers were not idle. She picked seeds from the cotton carried in her apron pocket, or knitted woollen socks for the soldiers.

A serene old age? She was perpetually anxious for the safety of her sons and her grandsons, all in the army. King and church, kindred, her country home, she gave up uncomplainingly. The sacrifice once made, she was thoroughly loyal to the cause of the colonies. A great calmness possessed her soul and shone in her face so that her friends noticed its beauty.

During the seven long years of the Revolution this mother saw her eldest son not once. But Fredericksburg was directly in the line of the couriers who rode from Williamsburg to headquarters. Constantly messages came to Mary Washington— of the army that was being created near Boston, of the seizing of Dorchester Heights, of the vote for the declaration of independence, of the defeat on Long Island and the marvelous retreat with George forty-eight hours in the saddle, of the Christmas party at Trenton, the brilliant stroke at Princeton, the sad, dreary months at Valley Forge, of the rejoicing when the French alliance was concluded.

Strong of will and firm of faith, she followed her son's career and the fate of the country, for the two were one. Always she watched and prayed. She would not listen to a word of complaint or despair. "Mothers and wives of brave men," she would remind her friends, "must be brave women."

The people gathered at her gate when tidings came. Calmly she read them the news. Betty Lewis would be all excitement.

"The sister of the commander," her mother chided, "should be an example of fortitude and faith."

Friends congratulated her on her son's splendid generalship. She remarked quietly, "George seems to have deserved well of his country." They showed her letters filled with his praises. She shook her head. "Nay, my good sirs, here is too much flattery, too much! Still he'll not forget the lessons I taught him. He'll not forget himself, though he's the subject of so much extravagant praise."

Once during a period of great anxiety a courier brought her a packet from headquarters. Dismayed he saw her drop it unopened into her deep apron pocket. Bursting with curiosity himself and mindful of the crowd of eager people at the gate he ventured to suggest, "There may have been a battle. The neighbors would like to know, Madam." She fished up the packet, glanced over it and announced, "A victory! George generally carries through whatever he undertakes."

After years of hardship and struggle and suffering the message came telling of the surrender of Yorktown. "Thank God!" fervently said Mary Washington, "thank God! All the fighting and killing are over. The war will now be ended. Independence and happiness will bless our country."

Cornwallis had surrendered! In front of her quaint, low cottage friends and neighbors gathered to rejoice with Mary Washington. An orderly dashed up, dismounted and touched his three-cornered hat.

"Madam——Madam," he cried breathlessly, "His Excellency will be here within the hour!"

"His Excellency!" she echoed. "Tell George I shall be glad to see him." And turning to her wide-eyed little servant, "Patsy, bring me a white apron."

Entering the town Washington left his staff of French and American officers. Alone he walked to his mother's house. With a warm embrace she welcomed him. She called him not general, but George. Noting the lines of care and responsibility those seven years had marked on his face she asked about his health. Of old times and old friends they talked. Not a word was said of the war, of his glory and success.

Fredericksburg planned a splendid ball in his honor. The committee made a special request that Madam Washington should come.

"My dancing days are pretty well over," was her

answer. "But if it will contribute to the general pleasure I'll attend."

The town hall was hung with flowers and evergreens. It was blazing with lights. The glittering French uniforms and the gala dresses of the ladies made a splendid picture. Leaning on her son's arm Mary Washington entered. She wore a plain black silk with snowy kerchief and cap.

A sudden silence fell on the assembly. From the door to the platform a path was opened. Every person bowed, the titled and courtly foreigners with incredulous amazement, the people of Fredericksburg with affectionate reverence, as with quiet dignity and graceful, unaffected manner she advanced and took her seat.

The distinguished guests could compare her only with a royal mother in Europe. Was this Madam Washington, the mother of the general? No diamonds? No lace and feathers? No velvet and brocade? The first shock of wonderment over, they crowded up around her to pay their attentions.

For two hours she held her court. She watched the dancers in the stately minuet. At ten o'clock she motioned to her son.

"Come, George. It's time for old folks to be at home."

Smiling a good-night to all she left the room. This was her only appearance in public as the mother of a hero. As the doors closed behind her one of the Frenchmen exclaimed enthusiastically, "Mon Dieu! If such are the matrons of America she may well boast of illustrious sons!"

About three years later, in sacque and linsey-woolsey skirt Mary Washington was raking up dry weeds and sticks in her garden.

"There's my grandmother, sir," she heard a childish voice call out.

She glanced up to see the little Lewis boy pointing her out over the fence. He unlatched the gate and came down the path with a tall French officer. She dropped her rake. The visitor bowed low. It was the Marquis de Lafayette. Did she know that he had made a special trip from Mount Vernon to Fredericksburg to pay his homage to the mother of his friend and say farewell?

"Ah, you've come to see an old woman," said Mary Washington simply, taking his hand. "Come in. I can make you welcome without changing my dress. I'm glad to see you. I've often heard George speak of you."

She took off her plain, straw hat and sat down opposite him, straight as a young girl, never touching the back of her chair. Lafayette spoke of the happy results of the war, the fine prospects for America's future. The mother listened calmly to the praises poured out by the marquis. The miracle of the age he called Washington, a greater general than Cæsar.

"I'm not surprised," came her brief answer, "at what George has done. He was always a good boy."

"Will you give me your blessing?" asked Lafayette humbly. "I'm going back to France."

She folded her hands and prayed that God would grant him

safety, happiness and peace. With tears in his eyes he bowed once more in taking his leave and kissed her hand.

"I have seen," he said to his friends, "I have seen the only Roman matron living at this day."

And indeed isn't this Mary like those women in ancient history who brought up their children to serve Rome? Cornelia said, "These are my jewels." Mary Washington might have said, "This is my life-work," referring to her children, all filling their places in life in a manner honorable to themselves and to her, and particularly her eldest son, the saviour of his country, applauded and revered by the whole world. Always her one ambition was to be a good mother.

How proud she was when he rode over with the news that he'd been elected president of the new United States! The day before he started to New York for his inauguration he paid this visit. He spoke of returning as soon as possible.

"No, George," she said quickly, "this is our last meeting." Well she knew that the disease from which she had suffered for three years must soon end fatally. Reaching up to lay her hand on his shoulder she added, "Heaven's blessing and a mother's benediction will always go with you."

He stooped down and put his arms about her. Into her hand he slipped a purse filled with gold pieces.

"But I don't need it, George."

"For my sake, Mother," he begged. So she kept it.

Four months later Mary Washington died. She was buried on the Lewis grounds, in a beautiful spot she had herself selected. On the day of the funeral all business stopped in Fredericksburg. Shops and houses were hung with black.

Over the whole country there was mourning. Newspapers and ministers noted the event. Members of Congress, says tradition, wore crêpe for thirty days as for a distinguished official. A great citizen of the nation had passed away.

"No fame in the world is purer than hers," the people said. "No woman since Mary, the mother of Christ, has left a greater claim to our love and reverence."

President Washington planned to erect a monument over her grave, but took no steps in the matter when Congress claimed that privilege. With all the work and confusion of establishing a new government this project was never carried out. Bills introduced asking for the appropriation were lost by various misfortunes. The country was content to glorify the son, toasting his name at annual banquets. The forlorn, neglected grave of the mother was marked only by a small headstone and weeds.

Years later a rich New Yorker heard that the people of Fredericksburg were trying to raise money to build this monument and offered to give the sum needed. With parade and ceremony the cornerstone was laid by President Jackson who described the spot as unmarked, but not unhonored. The base was completed, the shaft was brought ready to be placed in position, but—the work was never finished.

Did the New Yorker lose his fortune in the panic? Were the funds deposited in a bank that failed? On the death of contractor and stone mason was there no one to finish the monument? The shaft lay on the ground. The foundation stones crumbled and fell. Frost and water worked their ruin. Nothing was done year after year. Nobody seemed to care.

During the Civil War soldiers of North and South fought near this spot. In full range from Marye's Heights, the base of the monument was battered by cannonading. Following the ravages of battle came souvenir hunters who hacked and scarred it.

When the centennial of the United States was approaching plans were made for observing the anniversary of our first president's inauguration. Side by side with this news a Washington paper printed an advertisement of the sale of property in Fredericksburg. The house in which Mary Ball Washington lived and died, her grave, the monument material and some acres of ground were to be sold at public auction—in the city planned by her son and named in his honor, almost in the shadow of the Washington monument.

Everywhere patriotic men and women denounced this outrage with an outburst of indignation. One Virginia lady did something more. She wrote to the newspaper suggesting that American women contribute to erect a suitable monument to Mary Washington, because of whom she **was**, because of what she was. How better observe the centennial? Her dollar was sent to start the fund.

It was an enormous piece of work for women to undertake. The sum needed ran up into the thousands—to purchase and beautify the ground, erect a monument, and provide for its future care. They set to work with unbounded enthusiasm and energy. Committees of the Mary Washington Association were formed in every state. They asked for the pennies of the poor, the generous gifts of the rich. Every woman, every girl bearing the name Mary was urged to give something. Lectures and concerts, garden parties and colonial balls helped to raise money.

In 1894 in that beautiful spot in old Fredericksburg which Washington's mother had chosen, the plain monument of marble was dedicated, the first ever built by women in honor of a woman. Around it were planted willows from the tomb of George Washington at Mount Vernon. On one side are the simple words:

MARY
the mother of
Washington

and on the other:

Erected by her countrywomen.

THE MARY WHO TRIED TO BE FRENCH

Marie Antoinette: 1755–1793

"OH, my dear, if I could only keep you with me for always!" The empress sighed as she took her beautiful daughter in her arms. "Antonia dearest, think of me when misfortune overtakes you."

Why was she so anxious?

Did she remember that the girl's birthday was the day of the great earthquake at Lisbon and that her ambassadors, sent to ask the king of Portugal to be godfather, returned with sad news of the destruction of the city and the death of thousands of its people?

Was she afraid now that her plans might somehow fail? For years Maria Theresa and her ministers had been scheming to arrange a great match for this youngest daughter—nothing less than a marriage with the dauphin of France. "A lily for a lily," they bargained, giving a beautiful girl and getting for Austria the friendship of her old enemy. For so long the two peoples had been hostile that it had become a tradition. Now beside their own banners would fly the French flag with its golden lilies.

Like her mother's daughter the girl bore herself as they went into the throne room of the palace in Vienna. All the courtiers, the bishops and nobles, the deputies bowed low as the two advanced to the table to sign the papers spread before them. The empress was so moved that her hand shook. She could scarcely guide the pen. The daughter signed in a careless scrawl: MARIA—as the Austrians spell the name Mary—MARIA ANTONIA JOSEPHINE JOHANNA OF LORRAINE, ARCHDUCHESS OF AUSTRIA.

For the future queen of France her handwriting was as amazing as her ignorance; nay more, mortifying. Yet the girl was not altogether to blame. Her mother was very busy with the affairs of a great empire to supervise. Austria's many enemies were always plotting to rob her of her territory. The children were turned over to nurses and governesses.

Once in ten days or a fortnight the empress visited nursery and schoolroom and asked about the progress of her sons and daughters. In much the same way, less from love than from a stern sense of duty, she inspected the state hospitals and her military schools. Strict she was and dismissed in a hurry a governess who passed off her own writing, her own sketches as the work of Maria. The busy mother praised the child till she discovered the fraud. Her little daughter could scarcely read or write!

The next teacher was so fond of the girl that she never had the heart to correct her. A kiss, a laugh—and the merry archduchess went scot-free.

"The child's so clever," argued the governess, "she can do without learning lessons like other girls. And besides isn't she a princess? What need has she to be always poring over A B C's?"

So Maria learned little, for she liked neither books nor study. She was never forced to fix her attention steadily upon anything. She was never made to do that which she did not like. All her life long she wrote abominably. Many a peasant child knew more of geography and history than she. But to balance her education, or the lack of it, the fairies gave her two great gifts—charm and grace. These she had so abundantly, along with ready tact and sympathy, that everyone loved her.

When Maria Antonia was about eleven years old a brilliant French woman came to visit in Vienna and was introduced at court.

"What a charming girl!" she cried when she saw this youngest daughter of the empress. "I'd like to take her back to Paris with me."

"Take her, by all means," replied Maria Theresa. "I should be delighted." For the marriage of her beautiful Antonia to the French heir was the dearest wish of the mother's heart.

Home again in Paris the traveler spread abroad reports of the charming Marie Antoinette, as they said her name in French. All the court became interested in her. The king sent one of his best artists to paint her portrait. It was sent back to Versailles almost before the canvas was dry, so impatient was he to see it.

The wrappings were pulled aside. Louis XV was delighted with the beauty of the picture, and he was a good judge of beauty. From that day he was anxious to have his grandson marry this charming Austrian. So it came about three years later that the papers were signed and the empress made ready to send her daughter to Paris.

"How glad I'd be if I could keep you with me for always and always! But I must sacrifice my feelings for Austria. This marriage will help our country. It will make you happy too, I trust. Write me often—I'll weep over your letters."

Once more she took Maria Antonia in her arms. She could not let her go.

"Think of me, dearest, when misfortunes overtake you."

At last the girl tore herself away and hurried from the castle to the coach that was waiting in the courtyard. More than once she put her head out of the carriage window to look back at the home she would never see again. The tears rolled down her cheeks.

"Good-bye, good-bye, our archduchess!"

The streets were so crowded that the horses could hardly get through. All the people loved Maria. There were tears and lamentations that she was leaving Vienna, though they knew she was making a brilliant match.

" Good-bye, good-bye! "

The girl sat very straight and looked out at the blurred mass of faces. She smiled mechanically as she'd been taught to do. All her life she'd been told that the very sight of royalty was enough to make the common people happy.

On the Rhine, the boundary between France and Austria, a splendid pavilion had been erected. Here the Viennese ladies-in-waiting who had brought her thus far kissed Maria's hand for the last time. She gave them messages for her mother, her brothers and sisters. Then with her charming smile she turned to the French ladies waiting to receive her.

" Forgive me. These tears are for my mother and for Austria, my country. From this moment I am French and I will not forget it."

A royal bride must receive her trousseau from France, an old custom dictated, and may keep nothing belonging to a foreign court. So the Viennese ladies-in-waiting took off Maria's garments and passed her over to the French ladies who redressed her in the most beautiful attire their kingdom could provide.

" I'm enchanted with her beauty," one of them whispered.

" How lovely our new dauphine is! "

" Her eyes are as blue as the waters of the Danube! "

Their comments were echoed by the people who lined the road all the way from the Rhine to Paris. The peasants

cheered as the coach drove by. Girls scattered flowers in her
path. Bells were set ringing, cannon thundered as she passed
under triumphal arches.

" When the dauphin comes to be king and she's our queen,"
people said, " all France will rejoice."

Excited and happy, Marie Antoinette smiled and bowed
and waved her hand. These men and women and children were
delighted with her beauty and her loveliness. If long tradition
made the French hate the Austrians, they had no enmity toward her. Why had her mother spoken of misfortunes?

In the forest of Compiègne the royal family waited to welcome her at the château. The king's minister bowed before
her as she left the coach.

" I shall never forget," she said to him graciously, " that it
is you who have made my happiness."

" And that of France," he answered, kissing her hand.

For the first time Marie Antoinette saw the king and his
grandson. This marriage had been planned by ministers of
Austria and France. Neither bride nor groom dreamed of
rebelling against it. No matter whether the young people
cared for one another or not!

Louis XV, now an old man of sixty, was as delighted as his
subjects at the sight of this young girl. He was charmed with
her gaiety and wit, with her beauty of face and pretty manner.
But the sixteen-year-old dauphin stood before her tongue-tied.
The speech of welcome he had learned was gone quite out of
his head. Awkwardly he bowed, shifting from one foot to the

other. A timid, fat boy, quiet and bashful, he made a sorry figure beside his gallant grandfather.

On to Versailles they drove for the wedding. The Swiss guards were drawn up before the palace and presented arms as Marie Antoinette approached the royal chapel. Like every French bride she signed the register—MARIE ANTOINETTE JOSEPHE JEANNE DE LORRAINE. Some of the courtiers sneered when they found a word misspelled.

Before the ceremony was over a dreadful storm broke out. The festivities planned by the king were spoiled. The people who had come out from Paris to see park and palace illuminated were drenched with rain. Frightened by crashing thunder and terrific flashes of lightning they fled in a panic.

Born on the earthquake day, thought the bride, married in such a storm, what next?

The fêtes at Versailles lasted a fortnight. The halls of the palace, the wide garden paths were filled with courtiers in extravagant suits and gowns glittering with jewels. Every night there were banquets and dances and concerts. In the park four million lamps were lighted. The wedding festivities cost twenty million francs, to be paid by the subjects of the old king.

Paris too wanted to celebrate this marriage and announced a grand display of fireworks. That all the people might see and enjoy, it was given in the great square called the Place Louis XV, the pride of Paris. Such a crowd came, such a mob of eager men and women and children that the police could not take care of them.

Suddenly a shriek was heard. A burning rocket fell on a wooden scaffold. Bright flames leaped up. Panic spread as quickly as the fire. Some people were pushed into the river, some were trampled in the mad rush to escape from the Place.

The bride and groom were just driving up when they heard cries of terror. They looked out on a scene of tumult and death. Marie Antoinette never forgot that picture. All the money she had was sent to the families in distress.

The praises and attentions of the king, his many presents brought the dauphine not friends, but enemies. His petted favorite Dubarry was jealous of the girl. His three daughters gossiped about her. The courtiers did not like her haughty manner, her frank speech. Talebearers were everywhere. If she smiled at some young noble a dozen people talked of it. They twisted her words till the most innocent remark had a different meaning. They described the simplest action and made it appear wrong.

Marie Antoinette wrote to her mother frequently, scrawling her messages at the last moment before the royal post left. Had she written earlier her mail would have been opened by spies. For at the court were many enemies of Austria, only too eager to wound the bride.

The main charge against her was that she was too fond of fun, too lively for the dignified, staid French court. And indeed it was very different from Vienna where simplicity was just then the fashion. In Versailles etiquette ruled. For every look, every gesture there were hard and fast regulations. From her lady-of-honor, a perfect mistress of this art of etiquette, poor Marie met constant rebukes.

"You nodded when a curtsey was required," she would remind and caution her charge. "You smiled when it was not seemly. You ought to have bowed in such and such a way."

"How tiresome! how exasperating!" the girl would say to herself.

She was as fond of pleasure and gaiety as the king himself. She loved to dance, to sing, to have lively fêtes in the gardens, to play like a child, to take part in theatricals. She was lonely, with scarcely one real friend. The dauphin had no social graces. He liked to make locks and spent whole days in his little shop, tinkering with his tools. He liked geography and would study globes and maps by the hour, or watch the heavens through a glass. With his wife he did nothing.

But if many of the courtiers were cold to her Paris was enthusiastic over her beauty and charm. She was used to crowds in Vienna, but never had she been so cheered as on her first appearance on the balcony of the Tuileries, the palace in the city.

"Huzza! huzza!" cried the people over and over and over. They marveled at her gay spirits. They called her queen of beauty.

"Don't put too much faith in the loyalty of Parisians," Maria Theresa wrote her daughter in answer to the letter describing this scene. "They're fickle. They throw old idols down to worship new ones."

Small wonder that the dauphine loved Paris and ran off to its gaieties, glad to slip away from the cold parade and the jealous tongues of Versailles. Louis did not realize that his wife was hungry for pleasure. But his younger brother liked dancing and often escorted her to masked balls in the city. Hidden by her domino she would mix with the people and talk freely as she never could at court. Yet men would always recognize her and word would be whispered about, "The dauphine is here to-night."

"Her husband neglects her," commented the gossips. "Where does she go, without him, dancing till daylight and getting home through a side door in the palace?"

The old king was taken ill with smallpox. A candle burning in the window of his room was to be put out to announce his death. In the courtyard messengers waited, booted and spurred, ready to start instantly to carry this news to the other courts of Europe. In his own apartment the dauphin paced restlessly up and down. His wife watched him anxiously.

"Louis," she whispered in a bewildered tone, "I feel as if the skies were falling ——"

Suddenly there was a rush of feet, a stampede coming down their corridor. The door was flung open. The grand chamberlain threw himself on one knee.

"The king is dead. Long live the king!" In France an ancient law said there must always be a king.

With noise and clamor the eager courtiers entered.

" The king is dead.   Long live the king! "

Louis XVI and Marie Antoinette knelt down in tears.

" O God," they exclaimed, " guide us, for we are far too young to reign! "

Louis was twenty, his Austrian wife a year younger.   They knew little of statesmanship, little of the real condition of their kingdom.   Why trouble their heads about money affairs: vast sums wasted on jewels and splendid robes and extravagant banquets, the people crushed by heavy taxes and groaning under their burdens, one bad harvest after another?   Versailles wasn't paid for and represented a debt of ten million dollars.   Crippled by long wars, France was in danger of bankruptcy.

" After us the deluge," Louis XV answered when told of the empty treasury.   Now that he was dead his grandson must suffer the consequences.

" Why not be crowned at Notre Dame in Paris? " asked the minister of finance.   " It will save us fifty million francs."

" No, no, I will be crowned at Rheims.   For centuries the kings of France have gone there to be anointed with the sacred oil."

In the early spring of 1775 the road from Versailles to Rheims was repaired by the peasants—forced labor for which they were not paid, which called them from their fields at sowing time.   There would be no harvest to reap.   Furniture, tapestry and splendid mirrors were sent from Paris to adorn the queen's rooms.   To accommodate her high head-dress a

THE MARY WHO TRIED TO BE FRENCH 77

special coach was built with carved panels and cushions of satin and gold.

"Her carriage," peasants said as they caught a glimpse of the riches of court life during the four days' journey to Rheims and shook their heads over their own famine fare, "her carriage seems to drive over men's bodies as they fall at their work in the fields. Bread is higher than ever in France. Louis is to have a new crown that cost twenty million francs."

A gay account of this trip to Rheims Marie Antoinette wrote to her mother, telling of the coronation and the court ball, of the opening of the prison doors, of her husband's touching thousands of sick persons, of the people crowding around her coach to acclaim her. But under their cheers there were sullen mutterings. A storm was coming. Think of me, the empress had said, when misfortune overtakes you.

Queen now instead of dauphine, Marie Antoinette plunged into a round of pleasures and gaieties. She would submit to no restraints. She had her own way, but this way made her only more enemies. Little by little she lost her popularity with the people as well as at court.

The winter of 1776 was unusually severe. There was great suffering in Paris.

"Let's have some sleighing as we used to do in Vienna," suggested the queen. The royal sleighs were old-fashioned and dingy. She ordered new ones, gilded, with crimson leather cushions and silver bells.

"Austrian sport," growled the people as she dashed by,

"Austrian sport when men are starving! It's all her doings. You can't blame the king. Did you hear what he said when his brother urged him to order a gilded sleigh? 'Those are my sledges,' and pointed to a train of wagons bringing wood for the poor. Ah, yes, the young king has it in his heart to help us."

When anyone complained of his wife to Louis his answer was, "Let her alone." He paid her dressmakers and milliners and jewelers. He gave her pocket money when she squandered her allowance at the races. Even when she interfered in the council chamber, insisting on the appointment of some favorite or the dismissal of a minister who suggested economy at court, the king said, "Let her alone." He made this same reply when she sent millions of francs to Austria. Somehow, sometime things would work out for France. He was so easy going, his mind was so sluggish, no wonder he admired the queen's energy and force as much as her beauty. He could refuse her nothing.

"I wish I had a country house," she said one day, "where I could be free from all the endless etiquette of court life."

Soon after he made her the most gallant speech of his whole life.

"You love flowers. I'll give you a bouquet of them—Le Trianon—entirely for your own private use. It belongs to you by right, for it's always been the residence of the favorites of the kings of France."

The little Trianon was a pretty, two-storied chalet in the park at Versailles. High hedges around its gardens gave it

MARIE ANTOINETTE WOULD WALK THROUGH ITS GROUNDS

Marie Laurencin. *Woman Beneath the Willow*

real seclusion. In a white muslin frock and plain, straw hat Marie Antoinette would walk through its grounds with a friend or with a single servant. With her children she would chase butterflies or pick flowers. She sewed under the trees. She fed her pet doves and hens. She preserved fruit and churned butter in the dairy house.

Sometimes she stayed at the Trianon for several days at a time. She poured afternoon tea for her guests. Everyone walked about and chatted informally. People even sat down in her presence. What happy times she had! Who would imagine she was queen of the most exacting court in Europe? Easy to forget that France was starving.

"How much does the Trianon cost?" men began asking. "One more extravagance of the Austrian! We have a mad-cap queen, for sure!"

Paris and the whole country were filled with tales of Marie Antoinette's waywardness and reckless spending. Did some hint of this reach her ears she would say, "What? People are discussing the cost of palaces and crown jewels and court festivities? How impertinent for them to meddle in matters with which they have no concern!" In all her life she never imagined that kings and queens were created for any other purpose than to live in luxury.

The people of France were nearing the end of their endurance. King and court, they began to think, were the sole cause of their wretchedness. Bread cost an enormous price and bakers' loaves were short weight. Men fought each other in the streets for crusts. For everything they blamed the queen.

A jeweler in Paris had made a beautiful diamond necklace of flawless stones, perfectly matched. Louis XV had not lived to bestow it on his favorite. To whom could it be sold? The jeweler besought the young king to buy it. But Marie Antoinette, prudent for once, said, " No, I have as many jewels as I desire. You'd better spend that three hundred thousand dollars on a frigate for your navy." The poor man appealed to the queen herself, but she would not listen.

Then a woman of the court, using a cardinal as her tool and a forged note supposed to be from the queen, obtained the necklace and sold it stone by stone in London. The jeweler asked for payment and the whole story came out. Marie Antoinette was innocent, but the people showered blame upon her. " Madame Deficit," they called her now.

The storm was coming nearer and nearer. With voices that grew louder and more insistent men demanded that the king summon an assembly of nobles, clergy and representatives of the people to remedy conditions in France. Instead of rights of kings and courtiers, all Paris began talking of the rights of men. Soon a blaze was kindled that swept over the city like fire through autumn leaves.

" Arms! Give us arms! " cried the mob and helped themselves from the royal arsenals. " To the Bastile! "

They forced the few soldiers defending that old fortress-prison to surrender. Stone after stone they tore down its frowning towers and battlements, symbol of centuries of injustice. Word of this was carried to Versailles that night.

" Why, why," said the sleepy king, tired out after the queen's fête in the garden, " why, this is a revolt."

" Nay, sire," said the duke who had ventured to waken him, " it's a revolution."

And revolution it proved to be, such a turning over of government and throne as the world has never seen. It was the day of reckoning at last, reckoning for taxes from which churchmen and nobles went scot-free, which the common people paid with the last of their harvests, with their very lives.

In Paris women and children stood in long lines before the bakers' shops begging for half loaves of bread.

" Let's go to Versailles! " someone cried. " Bread enough there and to spare! "

" On to Versailles! " the crowd of hungry women took up the word eagerly. " On to Versailles! "

In one moment they had formed in line and started. The few grew to three or four hundred, then to as many thousands. A strange procession it was that marched that twelve miles in the rain—burly fishwives, washerwomen with their knitting, fine ladies forced to leave their carriages and join the others, hundreds of weary, hungry women clamoring " Bread—give us bread! "

The king was hunting. The queen was at the Trianon. They were called back in haste by word of the threatening crowd about the palace gates.

"Take the children," Louis urged his wife, "and flee to some distant place of safety."

"No, no! In such an extremity nothing shall induce me to be separated from my husband. They seek my life, I know. But I am the daughter of Maria Theresa and have learned not to fear death."

From the palace windows they saw the disorderly multitude pouring along the broad avenues in an endless, dense mass. The king received a group of fifteen women, promised all they asked, and kissed the leader on the cheek. Heedless of cold wind and rain the mob settled down for the night by camp fires. Lafayette posted a guard and the royal family retired.

Alas, for peaceful dreams! Through a side door of the palace a prowling band of men broke in and made for the rooms of Marie Antoinette.

"Save the queen!" called out two of her bodyguard and gave up their lives in a vain effort to hold back the mob.

Marie Antoinette wakened to hear shouts, the clash of swords, the firing of muskets, the fall of bodies. Wrapped in a shawl she fled along the corridor to the king's room, found the door bolted, knocked frantically as the threatening cries sounded nearer and nearer.

"Where's the Austrian?"

"Madame Deficit—let her pay for our bread!"

Trembling, terror-stricken she stumbled over the threshold. She could hear the mob rushing into her room, with swords and pikes stabbing the luxurious bed where she had been lying.

Outside the palace the angry crowd demanded that she show herself.

" Step out on the balcony," urged Lafayette. " It's your only chance of safety."

With her two children she stepped out.

" No children—the Austrian alone! Away with the children! "

She led the dauphin and his sister back. Alone she stepped out again. Her arms folded, her eyes raised to the sky, fearless and proud, her mother's true daughter, she won the admiration of the motley crowd. One man raised his musket. His companion pushed it aside. With one voice the fickle mob shouted, " The Queen! Long live the Queen! "

" The king goes to Paris," Lafayette reported to her. " What will you do, Madame? "

" Accompany the king," came her proud answer.

Through rows of scowling men and women the royal family passed out to their carriage. Marie Antoinette glanced back at that splendid palace which had been the scene of such grandeur, such happiness. Did she know she was seeing it for the last time?

Never had she driven to Paris with such an escort. Before and behind, crowding up against the carriage were hundreds of starving vagabonds, men and women with every sort of weapon, yelling, cursing, singing insulting songs. They fired off their muskets, startling the poor queen and almost suffocating her with the smoke of powder. The heads of her two guardsmen, fastened on pikes, they held up for her to see.

"We'll have bread now," the wretched women shouted in tired, shrill voices, "plenty of bread and to spare. We're bringing the baker and the baker's wife and the baker's little boy!"

For seven long hours that bright October afternoon this drive lasted. It was twilight when they entered the gates of Paris. With mock respect and ceremony the mayor received them and conducted them to the Tuileries. At every entrance soldiers were posted, nominally for the protection of the royal family, actually to prevent their escape. The great palace was become a prison.

For weeks and months the storm raged over France. What should they do with their king and queen, the leaders argued back and forth. Friends plotted and schemed for their escape, but Louis XVI would do nothing to help them. His idea was always concession, to win back the love of his people by favors. Affairs would change for the better soon and harmony reign in France once more.

Again and again Marie Antoinette urged vigorous action. Into the mild, passive king she tried to put her own firmness and courage. She appealed to her brother, now emperor of Austria. He promised an army of thirty-five thousand. Over the frontier the exiled nobles were assembling. Use force on such rebellious subjects, why keep faith with them?

By June she won Louis XVI over to her plans—escape from

Paris, near the frontier surround themselves with loyal citizens, use foreign soldiers against the troops of the National Assembly, and far away from the scenes of violence in the capital adjust all these difficulties. Arrangements were made with the greatest secrecy, but how could such strange plans succeed?

They must all travel in one coach, so a large coach was built and painted yellow. Troops must be stationed at every post where the horses were to be changed. Three guards must accompany them, dressed in livery. All this will attract attention, urged the king's friends. But he insisted.

About eleven o'clock one June night they started, slipping out of a side door of the Tuileries one at a time. The children's governess had a pass made out for a Russian baroness. The queen in gipsy hat and plain gray dress was their nurse. The king's sister was a maid, Louis himself a valet.

Their plans could not be carried out. Marie Antoinette lost her way and wandered about for an hour before she found the yellow coach. Harness broke and again precious time was lost. At more than one point no soldiers awaited their coming, so suspicious and hostile were the people.

The group in the coach were too frightened, too excited to talk. Through the dark hours they sat in silence grasping each other's hands. The children slept in the arms of nurse and valet. But as the day wore on the fugitives became less anxious. They drove through quiet, peaceful country.

" We're nearing the end of danger," they congratulated themselves, " the end of our sufferings."

By evening the king dared to show his face at the window of the yellow coach as he paid the postboys with fresh, new money. The picture on the bill, the face of this valet were the same. Louis XVI was recognized!

A mad ride of eighteen miles brought a young revolutionist to the next station for changing horses, half an hour before the heavy coach appeared. The bell was ringing the alarm. A cart was overturned at the bridge. The travelers could not pass. They must alight and take shelter in the house of a grocer, the mayor of the village of Varennes. The tired, sleepy children were laid down on the trundle-bed of the grocer's children.

Sitting on a box of candles Marie Antoinette pleaded with the mayor's wife to use her influence so that they could go on with their journey. A few miles further troops were assembled. At the frontier friends in great numbers would rally round them. Now she asked for pity with a mother's tears of despair. Again she begged for justice with all her queenly majesty.

" You're a mother, a wife. In your hands is the fate of another wife and mother. Think what I suffer for these two children, for my husband. The queen of France will owe you more than her kingdom, more than life itself! "

" Madame," said the grocer's wife coldly, " I'd be happy to help you if I could without danger. Hear the alarm bells! You're thinking of your own husband. I'm thinking of mine. A wife's first duty is to think of her own man."

Marie Antoinette burst into a flood of tears. Slowly the long hours of that wretched night passed. The ringing of the bells never stopped. Thousands of armed men assembled in the village. A few troops from a loyal regiment came up. Their captain offered to cut a way through and rescue the king. He refused to leave the children and his wife.

Orders came from Paris that the royal family were to be sent back. What a humiliating trip was that return! Great crowds of people gathered along the whole route to see the yellow coach drive past. It was very hot. The roads were dusty. Two guards sat inside the coach so that it was crowded. Marie Antoinette took the little dauphin on her lap. His sister stood in front of her aunt. The king napped as they drove slowly along.

Nearly a week had passed since they left the Tuileries. They entered it now between long lines of soldiers—not their troops, but the republic's.

During that anxious night at Varennes the queen's hair turned from auburn to snowy white. She still hoped for foreign aid, still looked to see the white uniforms of Austrian regiments in the streets of Paris. Louis XVI would do nothing. He was busy with a new lock.

For the next year events came rapidly for Marie Antoinette and France. In August the Tuileries was stormed by a mob. The Swiss guards who presented arms at her wedding stood their ground till the last man fell. With not a moment to lose the royal family sought refuge with the National Assembly, listened to its speeches and debates, heard the king named Louis Capet, a prisoner, fallen from his high estate. They were lodged in comfortless rooms in the tower of the Temple, once part of the palace of the king's brother with whom Marie Antoinette had gone to masked balls. Louis was separated from his family. His wife was frantic. When misfortune overtakes you, her mother had said. Had she dreamed of this?

September came and news that the allies—Austria, Spain, Prussia, Naples, Switzerland—were on the way. In the queen's heart hope grew feverish. No one told her when the soldiers of France won a battle. The king was brought to trial, proved guilty of treason, of plotting with foreigners against the French. Death by the guillotine was his sentence after a day and night of voting.

Two short hours Louis was allowed to spend with his family. The children clung to him. Sister and wife sat on either side. For a half hour not a word was spoken. Passers-by heard the cries that pierced through the stone walls of the Temple tower.

" Time's up! " called the soldiers.

" I'll say farewell to you to-morrow," the king said gently, to spare Marie Antoinette the agony of a last meeting.

Early the next morning in the dull January dawn she heard footsteps passing up and down the Temple stairs. Without their telling her she knew Louis XVI had gone without a good-bye.

" Tell her," was the message the valet brought as he gave her the king's seal and wedding ring, " tell her that I leave her with difficulty."

All her hopes were fixed now on the little dauphin. Passionately she clung to him and to her daughter during those lonely days. No friends to visit them, no news from the outside world, spies on every hand, constant insults from their guards—all this she had to endure. Plots were formed for her escape, but she refused to leave the children.

Because of rumors that they were planning to flee the soldiers were ordered to take the dauphin to another floor of the tower.

" No, no, let him stay with me," implored Marie Antoinette. " He is not well. Let him stay with his mother."

" Show no mercy," read the orders. From her very arms they tore the boy away in spite of her shrieks and protests. " What's the good of all this noise? " they asked harshly.

One August morning at two o'clock they wakened her with a stern command to dress in haste and go to another prison. Through damp, slimy corridors, down dripping steps they led her to the iron door of her cell. Entering she struck her head against the low beam.

" Did you hurt yourself? " a soldier inquired.

" Nothing can hurt me now," replied the Queen.

The cell was damp and dreary, with scanty furniture and a mattress of straw. A window without curtains looked out on the prison yard. Two soldiers watched her constantly, even when she dressed or slept. Her eyes, once blue as the waters of the Danube, could not read in the dim light. She could not knit or sew as the guard refused to let her have needles lest she kill herself. Once she had had four hundred servants. Now she was all alone. When misfortune overtakes you, think of me.

In a few weeks came her trial, a mockery of a trial like that of Louis XVI.

"See how proud she is," cried the spectators. "Down with the Austrian!"

"What is your name?" began the questions.

"Marie Antoinette de Lorraine," answered this Mary who had tried to be French.

"What is your condition?"

"Widow of Louis, king of France."

"What is your age?"

"Thirty-eight." Twenty years and more had passed since she came to Paris, a blooming bride greeted by the cheers of the people.

Forty-one witnesses were heard, questioned and cross-questioned. The diamond necklace, money sent to Austria, the flight to Varennes, her influence used to persuade the king to act against his subjects, plots for her escape—all this they touched on, but found it hard to convict her. In answer to a question about the dauphin she cried out, "I appeal to every mother here!" and hearts not tender melted at her words.

During the long hours of the hearing, till midnight and all the next day, Marie Antoinette did not hope for life. What had she to live for now?

"Have you anything to say?" one of the judges turned to the prisoner.

"I was a queen and you took away my crown, a wife and you killed my husband, a mother and you deprived me of my children. My blood alone remains. Take it, but do not make me suffer long."

Death by the guillotine was the verdict of the jury.

Marie Antoinette dressed herself in a flowing robe of white. She had new shoes, dainty, high-heeled shoes, a sad contrast to the old ones she patched herself in prison. Beneath her widow's cap strayed a few white locks—all that was left of her glorious auburn hair.

In a wretched, open cart, her hands bound, Marie Antoinette rode to the guillotine that rainy morning. Instead of cheers she heard jeers and insults from the people. That same hateful cry they shouted, "Down with the Austrian!" When the cart jolted and she lost her balance the women cried, "These are not the cushions of the Trianon!"

Upright she sat and calm till the Tuileries came in sight. There she had once lived in state. There in the garden her little son had played. The tears trickled down her cheeks. Then she regained her composure and with an air of majesty looked around on the crowd gathered in the Place de Louis XV where the fatal fireworks had been set off in honor of her marriage. There the guillotine had been erected for Louis XVI. And now ——

Up the scaffold steps she went, a tall, imposing figure. Accidentally she stepped on the foot of the executioner. With all the grace with which she would have apologized to a noble at Versailles she said, " Pardon me." Then in a low voice she added, " Make haste, for I'm alone on earth."

When he had done his work a few in the crowd rejoiced and shouted, " Long live the republic! " Others shuddered at the deed that was accomplished that day. The body of the queen was placed in a pine box and hurried off to an obscure burial. On the records of the cemetery of the Madeleine was written, " For the coffin of the Widow Capet, seven francs."

Beautiful, unfortunate Marie Antoinette Josephe Jeanne de Lorraine, archduchess of Austria, queen of France!

SISTER AND BROTHER

Mary Lamb: 1764–1847

WHEN you go to London one of the places you'll be sure to visit is the Temple. Pass under the archway and find yourself, after the roar of the Strand and Fleet Street, in an oasis, a green oasis in the dull grayness of murky London. It's a retreat as sheltered as a cloister. On every side dreary gray buildings wall it in, this Temple that isn't a real temple at all, but got its name because the Knights Templar built a church there.

In all the years of its existence more than one famous person has lived in the Temple. But your visit will be made because it was the home of a sister and brother.

In Crown Office Row in the Inner Temple there lived a poor lawyer's clerk and his family—wife, son John and little Mary. A shy and serious child she was, walking through the Temple garden, always too busy to play. Caresses and loving words

93

she seldom had from her mother, only coldness. Sometimes Mrs. Lamb would not speak to her daughter from morning to night. Add to this the fact that they were in very humble circumstances. The world seemed full of troubles to the sensitive child. No wonder that she often cried herself to sleep.

When Mary was ten a great, great happiness came to her. Into their rooms in the Inner Temple came a baby—a tiny baby brother. All the love in her heart Mary poured out on this brother. Babies are troublesome and take so much time and care, especially in a poor family with no servants. Never once did Mary Lamb think of little Charles as troublesome.

She was just old enough to be trusted with him. She would carry him down to the fountain where the sparrows splashed and washed just as they do to-day; and into the quaint, round church built by the Templars, where you can still see the figures of the crusaders carved in stone; and through the Temple garden where they could look right down to the Thames and watch the boats go past with the tide.

All her thoughts she whispered to him. The very best of care she gave him, for he was a puny little fellow. When he grew up how rich was her reward! This debt to his sister Charles repaid with a love so deep and strong that even the strain of a terrible tragedy could not break it.

Mary was never away from her charge save when she went to Fetter Lane for lessons. The school was for boys in the mornings, for girls in the afternoons. Over the door was a sign, " Mr. William Bird, Teacher of Mathematics and Lan-

SHE WOULD CARRY HIM DOWN TO THE FOUNTAIN

guages." But in spite of the fine sign both boys and girls learned only the three R's.

Mary helped with the housework and did errands for her mother and took care of her brother. Just one outside pleasure there was in her life. One noon she carried her father's dinner to Mr. Salt's office. Mr. Salt was the bencher for whom her father worked.

"You're a fine little girl," said he. "Do you like to read?"

"Oh, yes, sir." Then remembering, Mary added, "If you please!"

"Ha, ha! Take any book of mine. You're welcome to read here."

Many a happy hour she spent browsing in his library. All the good old English books she found and read whatever she would, with no one to choose for her, no one to prohibit. This was the best part of her education. It must be shared with Charles. He was only three when she taught him his letters. So skilfully she drilled him, with so little effort he learned that when he was older he used to say, "I didn't learn to read—I could always read!"

Charles, the sister felt, must have a real education. She ventured to ask Mr. Salt how it could be managed. Finally it was arranged that he, the bencher, would vouch for the boy's character and he should go to Christ's Hospital. The Blue Coat School! Mary held her breath when she heard this wonderful piece of news. Charles a Blue Coat boy!

She knew about that famous school. Two days before he

died the boy-king Edward VI had founded it for poor boys. Yet it had no hint of charity, for all the pupils felt proud to belong to a school as honored as it was old. Did king or teachers guess how many in its list of poor boys would later become famous, so famous that they made the school famous too?

Often Mary had seen these boys who looked as if they'd stepped right out of a book of costumes. They wore blue coats, with the long tails tucked up to the red belts for play time, bright yellow stockings, and a broad white band instead of a collar—the very dress worn by Edward VI and never changed in the school from that day to this. And now Charles Lamb, her brother, was to be one of these blue-coated boys.

Seven years old he was, but small for seven, with a slim little body and spindly legs and arms. Worst of all he stuttered and was never sure of getting through a sentence. The sister knew how timid and shy he was. With hundreds of rough boys, all bigger than he, all older, what chance would he have?

Well, he should never feel lonely. He should never forget that she was at hand. Every morning at ten minutes after eleven she used to leave her work and go down the street and watch for him through the iron bars of the fence. Mary would wave a corner of her shawl and Charles would wave back. When the bell rang and the boys marched into the building Charles held one hand high above his head that she might see it as long as she could. " All's well! " it said.

" Who's that girl, always hanging around you? " a tall, handsome boy asked Charles one day.

" Wh-why-why, that's my sister Mary."

" How should I know? "

So the next morning at ten minutes after eleven the two went down to the fence.

" Don't run away, Mary. I want to introduce someone to you. This is my sister, and this is Samuel Taylor Coleridge, but in school we call him Ajax."

What an evening it was for Mary when Coleridge called at their house! Her father recited poetry and played the harpsichord, a second-hand one given him by Mr. Salt. The brilliant, witty Coleridge argued against the whole family and talked them into silence and took snuff and flashed at them conundrums none of them could guess. He quickly won the brother's friendship at school. He was as quick to discover the sister's fine qualities and took her into his brotherly heart. Friends the three were to the end of the chapter.

Till he was fourteen Charles stayed at the Blue Coat School. Then, not because his education was finished, but because his earnings were sorely needed, he went to work in the offices of the South Sea Company, where his brother John held a good position. When the South Sea bubble burst, through Mr. Salt's help he became a clerk in the East India Company. There he toiled, sitting on a high stool, writing with a quill pen long columns of figures, long lists of indigo and tea for more than thirty years.

Monotonous work it was and rather poorly paid. But where would the Lamb household have been without that hundred pounds a year? The father had lost his place and was entering into second childhood. The mother was paralyzed and almost helpless. Old Aunt Hetty Lamb had such a tiny income that she made only one more to be fed and clothed. Truly it was no slight burden for Charles. His brother John was doing well in the world and had only himself to support. So he cared only for himself and left his family to its fate.

Nor was it a pleasant household for Mary to live in day after day, month after month. It was a nerve-wearing, indoor existence—housework, sewing, sewing, housework without ceasing, with never a good night's sleep, for the mother needed constant care. Against sickness and old age and helplessness Mary made her way. She was always overworked and nervous, always burdened with the sorrow of the family, always pinched by poverty.

And to balance this monotonous life she had no outside pleasures. Charles was gone from the house all day. Coleridge whose coming was enough, she used to say, to wind them all up and set them going again, was traveling on the continent. Only sick and helpless people she saw.

"What a queer person that Mary Lamb is!" said the neighbors. "Is she quite right in her head, do you think?"

No, something was wrong with Mary. At times she was conscious of a flightiness in her poor head. When she was a little girl her grandmother used to say, "What are those poor, crazy, moythered brains of yours thinking always, Polly?" Did she ask herself that question sometimes now when she was over-burdened and overwrought?

John Lamb met with a serious accident. He'd taken him-self and his earnings to more comfortable quarters. Now he returned home for his sister to nurse him. Father, mother, aunt, cooking, sewing—and now her older brother. This was the last straw!

They noticed one day that Mary didn't seem well. She'd been acting strangely of late. Could these be signs of insanity? Charles went for a doctor, but failed to find him in. In a sud-den rage gentle, kindly Mary Lamb snatched up a knife from the dinner table and stabbed her mother to the heart.

In the next room Charles heard the commotion. He rushed in, took the knife from his sister's hand, put his arm about her, and gently led her away. Their mother was dead. He could do nothing more for her. He shut the door to keep out curious neighbors. What could he do for his poor sister?

"Insanity," said the coroner's jury. "She must be sent to an asylum."

"Never," resolved the brother, "never in all the world!"

He made arrangements to have Mary cared for in a private house in Islington. The woman and her daughter became very fond of this new patient. She was not violently insane, but gentle and serene. They found presently that her attacks were fitful, coming and going. She need not stay there if the family would care for her at home.

Brother John was well-to-do in comparison with the rest of

the Lambs. What did he offer in this emergency? Nothing.
It was Charles who volunteered to be responsible for poor
Mary. And this meant no easy managing. Her care would
take fifty or sixty pounds a year. With his salary, the father's
little pension from Mr. Salt, and Aunt Hetty's tiny income
they could muster a hundred and seventy pounds, perhaps even
a hundred and eighty. Somehow they would make this do.
Have his sister in a public asylum?

" I'd rather die over a slow fire! " exclaimed Charles.

Gone was his dream of happiness with Alice W, the Alice
with blue eyes and bright golden hair. Gone was his dream
of marriage and living happily ever after. He might have
thought only of himself like his selfish brother John. Instead
he thought only of his sister.

" I must care for Mary. She is older and wiser and better
than I. Whenever I can I must live with Mary."

So he burned the diary he had kept about his love, burned
the poems he had written to Alice, but never sent. For more
than thirty years he devoted himself to his sister. Tenderly
he cared for her. All his money he shared with her. To keep
her laughing he joked with a perfectly serious face, even when
his heart ached at the thought of her terrible tragedy.

After three years the old father and old Aunt Hetty died.
Then Charles brought Mary home from Islington. Over them
hung the shadow that never lifted. Life was never free from
anxieties. Yet they had a vast deal of comfort together, this
brother and sister who were so devoted to each other. They

made the most of Mary's good months even though they were on the edge of poverty.

They moved frequently, for wherever they went the story of their tragedy followed them. They could never hope to avoid gossip in a village, but thought they might succeed in the bustling thoroughfares of London. But before they'd been long in a place, someone was sure to hear Mary's story.

" Yes, she's the one that ——" Charles would overhear one tenant telling another on the stairs.

" What—her mother? Did you say her mother? "

The landlord tried to explain why he needed their rooms. No use to argue the matter. Charles hunted up another lodging and would say to his sister, " It's too noisy here, Mary. I can't stand it! We'll have to move! "

They tried boarding, they tried lodgings in the country, they lived in half a dozen places in London. No matter where they were Mary's attacks of madness would come back. Sometimes they were caused by the fatigue and discomforts of moving and getting settled in a new home. Sometimes the brother was at a loss to account for them.

The shadows began to deepen. A strange look would come into Mary's eyes. When he saw it Charles would be deeply troubled. She was going to be ill again—not ill in body, but in mind. He learned to recognize the signs. Bravely dressed in his best suit he would put on airs as if bent on pleasure, and ask the East India House for a holiday. Were they thoughtful in that office and granted his request without too many questions?

A holiday? Charles would stay at home and try to cheer his sister. Sometimes he succeeded, for a time. Usually the shadow grew deeper and deeper. Then he would take her back to Islington. Across the fields they went hand in hand, the tears running down both their faces. There Mary would stay for a month, for six weeks, two months, the periods of her breakdowns getting longer and coming closer together as she grew older till she would be gone from home for four and even five months at a time. Charles would go back to his lonely lodgings to wait till she was better.

By day a bookkeeper, by night Lamb was a literary man. He wrote prologues, jokes (for three shillings a half dozen!), poems, a play, and the essays that have made him famous—essays done with such charm, such humor, such delicate fantasy, such a blending of laughter and tears that they've never been equaled. All the fun in his writing, the humor he put into his manuscripts and into his talk, he employed to make his sister laugh.

After a long day on his office stool he never failed to sit down to supper with some bit of fun he'd saved up to tell her.

"What do you think the Chief said, Mary? 'I notice, Mr. Lamb, that you come very late every morning.'"

"And what did you say, Charles?"

"'Yes, but just see how early I go.'"

She laughed till she cried when he told her that one of his

fellow clerks asked half angrily, " Pray, Mr. Lamb, what are you about?" and he replied, " Forty, next birthday." With a sober face he described the look of the lady who asked how he liked babies and he answered, " B-b-b-boiled, ma'am!" Coming back from a little excursion on the stage-coach, he was hailed by a woman who called out, " I say, are you full inside?"

" Yes, I'm quite full inside," he told her; " that last piece of pudding did the business for me."

Brother and sister, bachelor and old maid, they lived what Charles called a life of double singleness. In their shabby little rooms they were content with little, but wished for more. And lo! in the most surprising way their wish came true. Mary heard a cat crying behind the wainscoting. When her brother came home they tore away the paneling of the old house and pussy was released.

What a find for the Lambs! They discovered four rooms without a tenant, without even an owner who charged them rent. Little by little they took possession. Mary hung the laundry there to dry. Charles moved his bed into a larger room than the wee one at the top of the kitchen stairs. Because the visits of friends often interrupted his writing, Mary put a table and chair into one of these discovered rooms and proudly announced, " Charles—your workshop!" He tried for an hour or two to write there, but gave up discouraged.

" Mary, I can't work in that dull, unfurnished place!"

When he came home the next night he found strips of old carpet on the floor, and old prints put up on the walls. The print room, they called it at last, for they cut the pictures out of nearly all the books in their library and pasted them up on the bare whitewashed walls.

They hoped to make their fortunes out of Lamb's play, *Mr. H.* After many delays it was given at the theater. Charles bought the best seats for Mary to enjoy it splendidly. No, not the shilling seats in the gallery to which they climbed three or four times a year, but expensive seats in the very front. They joined with the crowd in clapping for an encore at the opening scene. Then they waited for the audience to applaud in good earnest. Before long people around them began to hiss and hoot. Fast and furious grew the hissing. Charles turned in, with Mary to help him, and hissed and hooted at his own play—lest people think they were friends of the author!

Even after the East India Company gave Lamb an increase of salary, they had a hard time to make both ends meet. Their friend Godwin suggested, and Charles eagerly seconded him, that Mary write herself. Why not do a book for children telling the stories of Shakespeare's plays?

"But Charles," she demurred, "I can't write. I never have."

"All the ideas I've ever had, Mary, are what you've given me. Begin and see what you can do."

Thus spurred on by poverty and by her brother, she set about her first literary venture. The *Tales from Shakespeare* was the work of both of them. Charles did the six tragedies, insisting that Mary mustn't have a thing to do with the sad stories that ended in death. The fourteen comedies were her part, to keep her mind on happy things only.

The preface too was a partnership. Mary did about two-thirds of it. Then as if she were utterly weary and out of breath and could write no more, her brother took up her pen in the middle of a paragraph—nay in the midst of a sentence, and carried it through to the end.

Does it seem an easy task to you, telling in prose the story of a long play in blank verse? Mary found many a difficulty as she read and wrote. Perplexing and unmanageable, she called the plots of some of the comedies. Putting witty dialogue into brief narrative required thought and care.

" Shakespeare must have had little imagination," she complained one day to her brother.

" Why, Mary? "

" Why, in *All's Well That Ends Well* he puts so many females into boys' clothes! This play teases me more than all the rest together."

But whenever she ran against a snag Charles would tell her how very well such and such a play was done, and flatter her into thinking she could get on with the difficult one in hand. Was it to encourage her that he often groaned over his own pages and said he could make nothing of them?

" He always says that," Mary told a friend, " till he has finished. And then he finds that he has made something out of it! "

The *Tales* were published in eight little pamphlets for children, at sixpence each. To the surprise of the authors they sold and sold well. Edition after edition was printed and eagerly purchased. Mary's share the first year was fifty pounds. She was very modest about her work, but time has tested it and it has stood the test.

Other writers have told these stories for young people. But in more than a century no book has succeeded in competition with the Lambs' *Tales*. Never has it gone out of date. In England and in America it has sold steadily, constantly, for each generation of boys and girls reads and enjoys it. What other book gives them so fine an introduction to the plays of Shakespeare? What tells his stories in a nutshell and makes them so alive, so fascinating? When I went to the bookshop to buy your copy, the clerk showed me no less than seventeen to choose from.

Did Mary Lamb never write another book? Yes, one for girls, called *Mrs. Leicester's School,* where on the first night at boarding-school each girl tells the story of her life. This too was a partnership book, for Charles wrote three of the stories. And in their third volume, *Poetry for Children,* there's no way to tell whether brother or sister is the author of a poem.

Whenever Mary was at home their friends came for the famous Wednesday evenings at the Lambs'. After the concert or the play they straggled in—the brilliant, dazzling Coleridge, and Hazlitt who quarreled with all his other friends, but could not quarrel with the Lambs, Southey, Wordsworth and his sister Dorothy, DeQuincey, Godwin—names famous in themselves, famous too as part of this circle.

Such gay talk and jolly teasing as went on during the games of whist or cribbage! The very best of talk, their friends said, with no ceremony and the least of expense. The center of all the fun was the little man with dark face and curly black hair, dressed in a black suit and black gaiters. Charles, they all called him, because he said Christian people ought to call each other by Christian names! Mary in her plain black silk dress and mob cap moved about quietly among the guests, with a smile as winning as her brother's. She listened more than she talked. Across the room she would help Charles out if he hesitated for a word.

About ten o'clock appeared Becky, the ill-tempered little maid, to spread the cloth for supper. Supper was always the same—cold meat, a great heap of smoking hot potatoes, and a vast jug of porter from the best shop in Fleet Street.

At last with the money from their writing, with an increase of salary, the Lambs were no longer so pinched by poverty. They had more than they needed, such simple, plain, homekeeping bodies they were. The greatest pleasure in life, Charles used to say, was to do good by stealth and then get found out. But even their best friends had little notion of their charities.

A marvelously fine time they had giving away this money, playing that they were rich patrons! They would give to a beggar, not noticing the value of the coin. Did they see a lot of very poor, very hungry children looking into a cake shop, they'd go in, load themselves with cakes, and come out, Charles stuttering, "H-H-Here we are! Who s-speaks first?"

They all spoke first.

Brother and sister pensioned off some little old ladies. Thirty pounds a year to one of them who years and years before had been Charles's teacher. To a poor friend he said with a blush, "Do you know, I've made out my will and put you down for so much. So I might just as well pay it now."

While they were living in the country once for a few months they saw a little Italian orphan named Emma Isola. Mary and Charles loved her at sight. They decided to adopt her and take her to live in their home.

" She'll bring us sunshine and youth and that's what we need," they argued.

So Emma went to live with the Lambs and never did child bring more happiness to her parents than she brought to this brother and sister. They laughed at all her little pranks. They almost spoiled her with their open admiration.

Mary taught her Latin, with Hazlitt's son and her own namesake Mary Novello. She gave the children their first taste of Shakespeare. Did she guess how her reading of the *Tales* fired the ambition of one of her listeners so that years later, when she was Mary Cowden-Clarke, she made the famous Shakespearian concordance?

Always anxious about his sister, Charles arranged for her care if anything happened to him.

" Mary, you must die first," he said to her one day.

With a cheerful little laugh she agreed. " Yes, Charles, I must die first."

But their plan did not work out. A fall, a month's illness, and the brother died. Out of her very love the sister was content to be the one left alone.

With many periods of darkness Mary Lamb lived on for a dozen years. She was a pensioner on the kindness of others, though she never knew it. When she was herself she never tired of praising her brother Charles and of making excuses for Coleridge. She lived only in the past and its loving memories.

Partners in play, partners in friends and letters and books, partners in their writing, partners all their lives in grit and pluck, they were not divided in death. The sister was buried in the grave of her brother in the grassy churchyard of Edmonton. A plain stone marks the spot, to the memory of Charles and Mary Lamb, " restored by a member of the Christ's Hospital School."

Brother and sister in the Temple garden, at the fence of the Blue Coat School, going across the fields to Islington hand in hand, with the tears running down their faces, sitting at the same table writing their immortal *Tales,* she taking snuff and he praising her work, talking with their friends on Wednesday nights—where can you find such devotion as was shown by Mary and Charles Lamb?

IN A FASHION MAGAZINE

Mary Somerville: 1780–1872

"ALL that money wasted!"

Mary's mother turned to the father reproachfully. "She's had a year in that expensive boarding-school in Edinburgh, and what's it done for her?"

"I know," he agreed sadly. "I could hardly afford it on a lieutenant's pay. But I couldn't have my little girl growing up a perfect savage, not knowing how to write, and a tomboy besides! Call her in now and I'll give her a little test. Let's see if she's really learned nothing at all."

Mrs. Fairfax sent one of the boys down to the beach to summon Mary. She listened while her husband gave the child directions.

"Write a note to Lady Russell telling her that your mother is much better."

110

Could he have given an easier examination? He did not hurry her. But when Mary handed him the sheet of paper he tossed it over to his wife in despair.

" There! You see! " he exclaimed. " Her writing's abominable, just abominable! She can't put words together to make a letter. Why, she can't even spell the words! Mary, Mary, what did they teach you at school? "

" Why, I had writing lessons and French, and English grammar," Mary counted off on her fingers. " And then the dictionary, Father, we had that every single day."

" The dictionary? "

" Oh, yes. The teacher would announce a page and give us time to study it. We had to spell the words and tell her their meanings and recite them off just in the order they were printed —that was worst of all! "

" Well, can't you remember anything? What a big girl you were, Mary, before I ever saw you! Eight years old you were when my ship came back after the war with the American colonies was over—or states, I suppose we must call them now. You'd never been to school. You'd just run wild.

" You taught her to say her prayers," he turned to his wife, " and to read a bit in the Bible, and to stand up when you came into the room. I was shocked to find her so ignorant. Do you remember how every morning after breakfast I made her read aloud one of the *Spectator* papers? Long and dull for a little girl, she complained. But for me the listening was agony. How badly she read! Very badly indeed, with a strong Scotch accent so that even I could hardly understand her. Why, I thought Miss Primrose's school'd make her over."

" I'd have been quite content," said the mother gravely, "if she'd learned to write well and keep accounts. That's education enough for a lady. But all that money spent in vain!"

" Oh, don't send me back to Edinburgh," the child begged. " Oh, Father, it's so dreadful there! I was utterly wretched the whole time. There were so many strangers for poor timid me to meet, and all the girls were older than I. We were all afraid of the headmistress, she frowned so. And as if the lessons weren't hard enough, we had to study them in harness!"

" Harness?" repeated Lieutenant Fairfax.

" Yes—stiff stays, Father, with steel bands that pulled me back till my shoulder blades met." Mary's straight, sturdy little body jerked back into the required position. " And fastened on to those bands was a curved piece of steel that went under my chin like a collar. Only think of having to learn a page of Johnson's dictionary strapped in harness like that! Why, I cried every single day. The older girls were sorry for me and used to bathe my face so Miss Primrose wouldn't know how much I cried. Oh, school was nothing but sorrows and troubles. Don't send me back!"

Father and mother gazed at one another helplessly. Mary slipped out of the room and ran back to join the children on the beach.

A whole year wasted! A large sum of money! Nothing accomplished!

THE BEACH AT LOW TIDE FASCINATED THE CHILD

If only these discouraged parents could have looked ahead, if only they could have known how famous their daughter would one day be! But Lieutenant Fairfax would never have said that the *Spectator* which his light-hearted lassie read aloud so badly would be called a classic two centuries later—the very essays whose faultless English you'll study in high school. So how could he guess that books about the most difficult things in science would bear the name of this tomboy Mary, the most learned woman of her day, the greatest woman astronomer in England?

Home again from that dreaded boarding-school, Mary was like a wild animal released from a cage. Instead of constant restraint she had perfect liberty once more. She raced through the little Scotch village on the Firth of Forth with the pointer Hero. She wandered over the countryside. Though she wasn't in school she picked up knowledge on every hand.

The beach at low tide fascinated the lonely child. She spent hours on the sands studying shells and stones, looking at star-fish and sea-urchins, watching crabs and jellyfish. She loved flowers of every kind. She learned to know the birds by their flight. When the nights were clear and cold she watched the stars from the closet window. How full of mystery the heavens were! One day she would understand those mysteries, yes, and make others understand them too!

When bad weather kept her indoors she didn't know what to do with herself. She cared nothing for dolls. In their small library she found a copy of Shakespeare, the *Arabian Nights,*

Pilgrim's Progress, and *Robinson Crusoe.* To her surprise she found that she liked reading when it wasn't a punishment.

"This is all a dreadful waste of time," insisted her aunt. "The child sews no more than if she'd been a man!"

"How provoking!" said Mary to herself. "Grown-ups find fault because I read so badly, and then they find fault because I read so much. If it's wrong to get knowledge, why do I want it so? Is that just?"

To the village school Mary was sent to learn plain needlework. Was the aunt surprised when she proved an apt pupil? An old lady of the neighborhood sent some very fine linen to be made into shirts for her brother.

"I want Mary Fairfax to make one of them, all by herself," was her request.

When the shirt was finished, aunt and mother and the old lady inspected it. Mary had done her work so well that her days at sewing school were over. Instead she was given charge of all the mending for the household.

She did, however, have some hit-or-miss lessons. The village dominie, as the Scotch call the schoolmaster, came for a few weeks in the winter evenings. He showed her how to use two small globes she found—one for the earth and one for the heavenly bodies. How fine it was to look at the stars and then hunt out their names on the globe!

There was one person, just one, who understood her hunger for knowledge and encouraged her in her desire. This was her uncle, the minister at Jedburgh, in whose house she was born. In the early mornings they took long walks together whenever she visited at the manse. At last Mary found courage to tell him how she'd tried to teach herself Latin and could read in Cæsar's *Commentaries.*

" But it's all in vain, I'm afraid."

" Why? "

" What chance is there for me? Boys have every assistance in the world, and they spend years learning Latin. How can a girl by herself? "

" In years past some women studied Latin and made themselves real scholars. Some of them were of high rank. One was queen of England. Why don't you read Latin with me during this visit? Can you manage an hour or two before breakfast? Come to my study to-morrow morning and I'll start you on Virgil."

With still less encouragement and help Mary set herself to learning French when a cousin loaned her a French book. She used a dictionary and the grammar of boarding-school days. She used too all her persistence and kept at this task till she could make sense out of the story.

Then the family moved to Edinburgh in order that Mary might have social advantages. Now she had lessons aplenty— riding lessons, and cooking lessons with a famous chef, and piano lessons with five hours of practise each day, and dancing lessons on Saturdays at Strange's. Country dances, the minuet, the reel she learned. She danced so well and was so pretty that she never lacked a partner. The young officers from the Castle used to come down to Strange's and bring the girls gingerbread and oranges.

One more kind of lessons Mrs. Fairfax insisted that her daughter must have—drawing lessons from a landscape painter. A queer method he followed! His pupils looked on while he painted. Then he gave them a picture to copy and corrected their mistakes. Years later he said, " The cleverest young lady I ever taught was Miss Mary Fairfax."

But all these accomplishments had nothing whatever to do with her success. That she ever accomplished anything worth while was due not to these many teachers, but to her own industry.

Frequently she had to go to tea-parties with her mother. The buzzing talk of the older ladies did not interest her. But one red-letter day she met a young woman who spoke of a new kind of fancy-work.

" Come and see my things," she invited. " Can you, to-morrow? "

Mary went and admired the fancy-work at which her hostess was so clever.

" How is it done? Where did you learn? " she asked.

" In this magazine," and Mary was shown the book with colored pictures of dresses, with designs for embroidery and new crochet patterns. In the back of the magazine there were some charades and puzzles. At the end of one page her eye lit on a question in arithmetic. She turned the sheet and was surprised to see the strangest looking lines—figures and x's and y's all mixed in together.

" What's all this? " asked Mary Fairfax.

" Oh, it's a kind of arithmetic. They call it algebra. But that's all I know about it."

And they talked of other things.

Algebra! Algebra! The word had a fascinating sound. When she reached home Mary looked in all their books to find out what algebra was. There was no one she could ask. Her friends knew nothing of this, or any other science; and if they had known she hadn't courage to ask them and be laughed at for her pains. For months her question went unanswered. Algebra!

Then one morning, in the most unexpected of places, a helping hand was held out to her. The drawing teacher said to some of his older pupils, " You ought to study Euclid. That's the foundation for perspective and astronomy."

Was she better off, now that she knew the names of the books she wanted? It was impossible for her to go to a bookseller and ask for them herself. Secretly she begged her youngest brother's tutor to buy her an algebra and Euclid. Before she could start these fascinating lessons, she had to review what little arithmetic she knew. She recited to the tutor till she made sure she was on the right road. This was how she began the studies that were to bring her fame.

The five hours of piano practise, the painting and sewing she kept up without fail. The days were too short for all these tasks, for social pleasures and duties, and mathematics besides. So she sat up very late at night with her new books.

" It's no wonder, madam, the candles are used up so fast," the maids complained to her mother. " Miss Mary's are burned clear to the socket every morning."

" Take her candle away as soon as she's finished undressing," ordered Mrs. Fairfax.

But by this time Mary had finished six books in geometry. She continued to study till late at night, but without disobeying her mother. She solved a certain number of problems in her head every evening.

A gay, social place was picturesque Edinburgh. Pretty Miss Fairfax was a great favorite. Under the crags of the famous old Castle she promenaded. On Princes Street, the most beautiful street in Europe, she shopped with her girl friends and their dancing partners joined them. At the theater and for the stately minuet young men crowded about her. All her own dresses she made, even the fine India muslin frocks she wore to the balls. Apparently she led the pleasant, idle life of a young lady in society, for her father was now Sir William Fairfax and an admiral. But at dawn Mary wakened and quietly dressed. Wrapped up in blankets because of the cold she studied till breakfast time.

Her father had been home only a short time when somehow he found out what his daughter was doing.

" This won't do," he declared emphatically to his wife. " I must put a stop to this, or we'll have Mary in a strait-jacket one of these days. Remember poor Mr. X. who went raving mad about the longitude!"

At twenty-four Mary married Captain Samuel Greig, the Russian consul for Britain, and went to live in his bachelor's house in London. She wasn't at all happy. All day long she was alone and had to study as best she could. In her love of science her husband had absolutely no interest. He had no opinion of a woman's ability. What intellectual work could she do? All the prejudice of his age against learned women Captain Greig had to the full. He was annoyed to find his wife less stupid than himself! Not that he prevented her studying; but he gave her no encouragement.

After three monotonous years in a dreary London street Mary's husband died. She returned to Edinburgh with her little boy. Now for the first time in her life she could follow her natural bent. No longer must she solve problems by candle-light or shiver in the early morning. No longer must she secretly ask a tutor to buy her a book. She was free!

She subscribed for a mathematical journal and sent the editor her solutions to its problems. In return he sent her some of his. When he published a prize question and she answered it correctly she received a silver medal cast with her name. How delighted she was with this first honor!

Fortunately for her this editor was appointed professor of mathematics in the University of Edinburgh. Mary told him her longing to go through some regular courses and he gave her a list of the books she would need. Most of them were in

French or Latin, but that could not deter her. She bought this little library and at thirty-three began real study of her favorite subject. Was this treasure her own? She smiled as she recalled the mysterious word *Algebra* in the back of the fashion magazine.

Her relatives of course disapproved. Eccentric and queer and foolish, they called her because she went little into society. But now she cared not a whit for their censure and could afford to do as she pleased. With all her hours of study she watched over her son's education, managed her household carefully, and kept up her music and needlework.

More than one offer of marriage came to her during these years. One gentleman courted her for some time, then sent her a volume of sermons with the page turned down at a long discourse on the duties of a wife. She returned the book at once and—refused the proposal.

Later she married her cousin, Dr. William Somerville, in whose father's house she had been born. He was the son of the friendly uncle who encouraged her to study and helped her with Latin. This marriage was an absolutely happy one for Mary. For their wedding journey they took a trip to the beautiful English lake country.

Soon the doctor's brother and his wife and sister joined them. The party was detained for a month by the brother's illness.

" Oh, how I'd love to have some currant jelly! " he exclaimed one day during his convalescence.

" I'll make it for you," the bride offered.

" What? What? " her sisters-in-law cried in amazement. " Can you do anything useful and domestic? " For they'd heard of her queer tastes and took it for granted that she knew nothing about housekeeping. Indeed one of her new relatives, younger than she, had written to Mary, " The news of your engagement has just come. We all hope you'll give up your foolish studies and make William a respectable and useful wife."

But Dr. Somerville did not agree with them. He loved his bride. More than that, he appreciated her. " She's far superior to me," he said frankly. Instead of throwing obstacles in her way, he entered into all her plans and encouraged her to go on with her studies. His admiration for her work was unbounded.

Once they were settled in London he suggested her going to lectures at the Royal Institute. He urged her to take up new subjects.

" Use this chance and read Greek with your boy's tutor."

An hour before breakfast she read Homer, just as long before she had studied Latin in the early morning with her father-in-law. When she discovered that the tutor knew something of botany she began that too, though she was nursing a baby girl at the time.

Some of these new pleasures the Somervilles enjoyed together. They studied all one winter how crystals were formed, again how rocks were changed into soil. Together they made a fine collection of minerals and added to it on their travels in France and Italy.

"What extravagance!" said their relatives.

Certainly it was due to her husband that Mary Somerville began the work which was to make her famous. A great French astronomer had just died, LaPlace, often called "the Newton of France." He had written a famous book about the planets and the laws of gravitation. A learned volume it was, but Mary had mastered it with her usual perseverance and energy.

In Paris she had met the Marquis de la Place. She dined at his country house. He autographed one of his books for her. They talked together about astronomy.

"She's the only woman," he used to say, "who understands my work!"

All Europe was praising the great Frenchman. Yet not twenty men in England knew his book. Not a hundred knew it even by name. The work of a great genius, it was too hard for most men, even very well educated men, to understand.

If it could be translated into English and made simpler so that ordinary people could grasp it, how splendid it would be! Instead of twenty Englishmen honoring LaPlace, why not add ciphers and make it twenty thousand? Some men interested in the spread of science put the matter before Dr. Somerville, first by letter, then by a personal call.

"Will your wife do this? If not, it must be left undone. She's the only person who can write the book we want. Can't you persuade her?"

Mary Somerville was utterly surprised at this request.

"What a difficult task!" she exclaimed. "Why did they ask me? There are so many men, educated at the universities. Isn't it the height of presumption for me to do this book—or any other, William?"

But he begged her to try and finally she agreed.

"On one condition," she insisted. "It must be kept secret. Then if my work proves a failure, it can be put into the fire and no one be the wiser."

Now it's easy enough for a man, under plea of business, to plan his time and keep to a schedule; but alas! not for a woman. What if the mother was writing a book? All her every-day duties had to go on just the same. The servants must be given directions. The children's lessons, three hours every morning, couldn't stop. Music, Latin and Greek, algebra and geometry she taught them. The newspapers and all the most important new books she could not neglect. The evenings at home must continue, for the Somerville house was a favorite meeting-place for literary and scientific people.

All the time she worked at the translation and rewriting of LaPlace with giant understanding, this Mary neglected nothing. She was a good wife and a good mother, and a noted housekeeper as well.

"A scientific woman," she often said, "doesn't need to be a

slattern. Why should she be down at the heel or untidy in her dress? Why must she work in a dusty room?"

Successfully she balanced and combined the two—mathematics and all her daily tasks. A friend who was in the secret said, "Her head's among the stars, but her feet are firm on the earth!"

Just when she was in the midst of a difficult problem one of the little girls would ask, "How much's seven times nine, Mother?" or "What tense is this, with *ba?*" Patiently she answered and returned to her own thoughts. In the drawing of a complicated diagram she would stop to speak to her daughter touching a wrong note as she practised scales across the room. She taught herself to take up her work just where she'd left it, as you put a mark into a book and go right on with your story.

When the bell rang to announce a visitor she would hide her papers away in the table drawer.

"I've come to spend a few hours with you," the intruder would say with a smile.

"I'm so happy to have you," would come the gracious answer.

Did her husband protest against these constant interruptions she would say, "But William, when our friends come all this long way to Chelsea to see us, I can't refuse to see them!"

In less than three years her difficult task was finished. La-Place was ready to give to the every-day world. Diagrams and figures Mary had added. Problems she had worked out.

The text was remarkable for its clear arrangement and its simple, crisp style; and this, the critics said, was due to her enthusiasm for her subject.

Call it a failure? Put it into the fire? Scientists hailed the book with great applause. The whole edition was quickly sold out. The University of Cambridge made it a text-book.

"What a pity," one astronomer said, "LaPlace couldn't have lived to see this!"

"A woman's book," confessed another, "it puts us all to shame when we've been laboring in mathematics all our lives!"

"Your work," wrote one eager reader, "makes me feel like a boa-constrictor after a full meal. My mind is distended by the magnitude of the universe as you present it. I'd never dreamed our world was so immense."

At once Mary Somerville found herself in the front rank of scientists. Honors poured in upon her. Learned societies all over the world elected her to membership. When she traveled men of science entertained her and showered kindnesses upon her. England gave her a pension of three hundred pounds a year. Loudest of all in her praise were the relatives who'd scoffed at her and ridiculed her silly studies.

In the midst of all these honors Mary was modest and unassuming.

"I'm only an uneducated Scotchwoman who taught herself," she would say. "I'm afraid I'll use Scotch words and idioms without meaning to."

No one was more surprised than she at the success of her

book.   She liked all the letters of congratulation that came to her.   She liked sitting to the great sculptor, Chantrey, for the bust which the Royal Society of London voted he should make, to be placed in their great hall.   But most of all she liked her husband's pleasure and delight in her triumph.

" Not one man in ten thousand," she said to her children, " would rejoice as he does."

Dr. Somerville was ambitious not for himself, but for his wife.   He was proudest when the world showed its appreciation of her talent.   He was happiest when helping her.   He searched the libraries for any books she needed.   He copied and recopied her manuscripts.   He corrected her proof.

" No trouble is too great," he would say.   " It's all a labor of love."

For she did not stop with this one book.   When it was published she did not know what to do with all her spare time.   She had got into the habit of writing.

" I feel," she said laughing, " like a man thrown out of his job."

A sentence in the preface of her book on LaPlace gave her the idea for another work—a book to show how the different sciences are related.   A third book she did, and then a fourth when she was eighty-nine.   Constantly she planned for new editions to keep her writings up to date.   She saw them translated into German and Italian.   She saw a sixth, a ninth edition published in England.

Whether the Somervilles lived in London or Rome or

Naples, nothing was ever allowed to interfere with her morning's work. When a new edition of one book was called for, she was writing on another; but she put on high pressure and worked away at both.

"I'm afraid I'm getting behind in higher algebra," she confided to a Harvard professor whom she met in Italy when she was an old lady of more than ninety. "I've rather neglected it while I've been writing my popular books. Can you send me the very newest works in that line?"

She remembered her first x's and y's in the fashion magazine and smiled to herself. She was as delighted as a child when the box of books arrived from America. Every morning for three or four hours she solved the new and fascinating problems. She wrote slowly with a shaking hand. But if some x-y-z question proved difficult she'd attack it the next day and persevere till she had the answer.

Her own education had been up-hill work against enormous difficulties. She was eager to make things easier for other girls. She took great interest in all the efforts in England to improve their education.

"A woman's college is to be established at Cambridge!" she announced to her daughters with delight. "Only think all that that means! I want you to give my mathematical books to that college—those French and Latin books that made up my first little library—and the new books too, and my instruments."

One of the first of the women's colleges at Oxford was named Somerville Hall. In her honor was founded the Mary Somerville scholarship in mathematics, open to women only. And to-day young women winning honors in the sciences are carrying on the splendid work of this Mary who got her start in a fashion magazine.

MARY WITH THE GREEN VELVET BAG

Mary Lyon: 1797–1849

"WHAT are you doing, Mary? Come down at once!"
The busy mother stopped in the doorway, amazed
to find her little daughter standing on a chair by the
mantel with the hour-glass in her hand. What was the child
about? She ought to be spinning if the butter had been churned
and the cheese was set.

Mary looked at her mother with sober face.

"I can't come down. And I think," she added slowly, "I
think I've found a way to make more time."

Indeed this bustling household in western Massachusetts
needed extra hours in their day to get all the work done. There
were six girls and a boy and the mother, all to be supported from
a hillside farm. The Lyons were poor, but they weren't unhappy. The mother was a genius for making the most of

things. She was thrifty and taught her children thrift. Very early they learned to work and to look out for themselves.

There was so much to do! The wool from the sheep, the flax that grew in the meadow fields must be made into cloth and then into garments. Straw must be braided for new hats. Stockings and gloves must be knit. Fruits and vegetables must be dried for the winter. Little time had Mary to play, for she helped with all these tasks.

But out of doors everything was beautiful—the mountains and trees, the rocks and streams. From the top of the hill she could see Mount Holyoke standing like a sentinel on the bank of the Connecticut River.

"The mountains were my first teachers," she used to say years later. "The four seasons taught me patience."

Mary went to the district school two miles away. She learned to read and write and spell. But school lasted just a few months each year. This was only a reason for her to study harder, for she was a hungry little girl and couldn't get knowledge enough. She did her lessons faster than the others.

"May I study grammar?" she asked.

In four days she learned the whole book and astonished the teacher by reciting it from cover to cover.

"I'd like to see what she would do if she could go to college!" he exclaimed.

When the school was moved farther away she went to the little town of Ashfield for the winter. She did housework to pay for her board.

"Well, that Mary Lyon's a wonderful girl, isn't she?" some-one asked the man in whose family she lived. "They say none of the boys can keep up with her. But how is it now with her work? Does she really do anything or do you just give her her meals?"

"She wings the potatoes," was the answer. "And I assure you she does it thoroughly."

Nowadays we don't wing our potatoes, so you don't have that little task for yours. But when they were roasted in the ashes in an open fireplace, all the dust had to be brushed off with a turkey wing. And whatever Mary Lyon did all her life long she did thoroughly.

Every spare moment she spent over her books. When she was twelve she decided to be a teacher herself. Such a thing was unheard of! Girls of that day were supposed to grow up and be wives and mothers and housekeepers. No special train-ing was necessary for that.

Boys of course were different. They'd be doctors or lawyers or ministers. So they must go to school. The very first set-tlers in New England had been anxious that their children should be well educated. But to them children mean boys only. A girl didn't need Greek or Latin or mathematics to help her spin and weave and cook. So no girls went to college, nor even to grammar school.

"If a girl can read and write that's book learning enough," argued those good men. "And as for arithmetic all she needs is to know how many yards she'll have to spin to buy a peck of potatoes. Why, who'll cook our food or mend our clothes if females are taught?"

Like other girls of that period Mary Lyon had only a taste of education. But unlike them she was far from satisfied. Somehow she must earn money and have more schooling. Her mother married again and moved out west taking the younger sisters with her. Thirteen-year-old Mary kept house for her brother and did it so well that he paid her a dollar a week.

"I never saw such dollars," she described them long afterward, "nor have I since. I wept over them!"

She began to teach for seventy-five cents a week and her board. At first she failed utterly. It wasn't possible for her to keep order. She'd laugh with the children.

"If you commence teaching and don't succeed," was one of her sayings, "teach till you do. That's what I did."

Soon she became a very popular, as well as successful teacher. The families where she "boarded round" loved her so that each one would gladly have kept her for the whole term.

Whenever there was opportunity she'd seize a few weeks at school and be a pupil again. One teacher found her forging ahead of the class. He gave her a Latin grammar on Friday and assigned the first lesson. Monday afternoon she took her place on the center bench to recite.

All his questions she answered so promptly that the other pupils let their books fall in amazement. They leaned forward in their seats to listen and stare. Scarcely a slip she made through all those hard declensions and conjugations—amo and rego and princeps, principis and the rest. On went the questions and her ready answers till school hours were over and the sun dropped down behind the hills. For years the village talked of that recitation. No one could study like Mary Lyon. Think of memorizing Adams's Latin grammar in three days!

When she was twenty an academy was started at Ashfield. She determined to go. But how pay for her board? She counted over her possessions—a bed, some table-cloths, and two coverlets which she'd spun, woven and dyed herself. These she took to a boarding-house and bargained with the woman, giving them for a room and meals.

These were red-letter days for Mary. She might never again have such a chance for schooling. So she studied hard, ate her lunch in a hurry and slept little. She was intent on her books. She was so absent-minded that she'd leave off some article of dress or wear it wrong side out.

" Oh," she used to say to her friend Amanda White, " don't ever let me go down to breakfast without my collar!"

For the first few weeks at the academy she was very awkward and ill at ease. Her blue dress that she'd made herself, with a gathering string at the neck and wrists, made people laugh. But not for long was she a laughing stock. Not a pupil in the school could keep up with her. They all admired her without being jealous. For busy as she was she always had time to help them with puzzling lessons. She had so much charm and so merry a laugh that everyone liked her.

" That's the famous Mary Lyon," they pointed her out to

visitors, "famous for three things—for her homespun dress, her amazing mind, and her kindness."

Mary had saved money enough for only one term. She was planning to stop and teach again when Squire White persuaded the academy trustees to give her free tuition. She went to live at his house. Harder than ever she studied.

"Mary's fitting herself for some important station in life," Amanda told the family. "We must all help her."

"She's a brilliant diamond," the teachers commented to each other, "and only needs polishing. We must all encourage her."

Squire White decided to send his daughter to a new school at Byfield. There was much talk about it in their home. One day Amanda found Mary Lyon in tears. What was the trouble? She too wanted to go to Byfield.

"And so you can," said Amanda.

"Oh, no, I can't."

"Yes, yes! Talk to Father. He'll find a way."

And the good squire did. He lent her the money to be paid back when she began teaching again. Mary's other friends were all against this plan.

"You're twenty-four years old," they said emphatically. "You know enough already—more than a woman ought to know. It's not necessary for you to study more. For you'll never be a minister."

But she held to her purpose. And that summer at Byfield proved to be the most wonderful in her life.

" She's getting knowledge by handfuls," Amanda White described it.

But more than that Mary gained a new point of view. Always she'd been wrapped up in her passion for study. Eagerly she'd taken all she could get just for the pleasure it gave her. Now it suddenly came to her that nothing is satisfying or useful unless it helps others. The more she knew the more chances for usefulness would come to her. And this gave purpose to her life—service for others.

She taught in Ashfield in the winters, at a girls' boarding-school in Connecticut in the summers. In dealing with girls she was most successful. Her schools grew and grew. The pupils boarded in the neighborhood for a dollar a week. Tuition was twenty-five cents. Who could grow rich on such an income?

For years Mary had been teaching, moiling and toiling to get her own education. Little by little she worked out in her mind a plan for the training of girls. Her own had been irregular, hit-or-miss. She'd like a school with a course of study carefully planned for two years, or three or four, instead of a jumble of unrelated subjects. She'd leave out most of the extras of the finishing school—embroidery, music, drawing, manners, a smattering of French. She'd teach English and history, languages and science.

" If you want to have a good education," she'd say, " have a good foundation. Polishing a piece of sponge you'd find hard work, but not polishing steel."

School after school in New England Mary Lyon watched slowly build up a reputation depending on one person. With that teacher gone it would collapse and lose its influence. Schools were organized to make money exactly like a factory. Men took shares of stock and expected a good rate of interest.

"That's what makes the charges so high," thought Mary Lyon, "that only wealthy pupils can go. Now I want an education so good that rich girls can buy nothing better, while middle-class girls can meet its bills and enjoy all its advantages. For the middle-class is the mainspring and wheels that move the world."

Her own schooling had been grievously hampered by lack of money. For poor girls she had the tenderest sympathy. They were the ones who wanted education most and struggled hardest to get it.

"Now my school," she'd say to herself, "must have such low prices that farmers' girls and workingmen's daughters can come, and teachers who have to depend on just their own salaries. We must have a dormitory so the girls won't have to board out in the town. We can meet part of the expense by having them do the housework. This'll cut down the bills. And it'll answer the people who keep asking, 'Dear me! who'll make the puddings and pies when our girls are educated?' And it must have endowment so that my school'll be permanent and not fail if a certain popular teacher leaves."

For two whole years Mary Lyon thought over this plan. Daily she prayed over it. At last it took definite shape in her mind. She laid it before a committee of twelve men. They talked it over, voted for it and estimated the money needed.

"A thousand dollars we must have at once," they said, "to use in raising this sum. Then we can tell people that the expense for our agents who travel about getting subscriptions won't come out of what they give. Every cent will be used for the school itself."

Mary Lyon was teaching, but she promised to get that first thousand dollars.

"And all from women!" she said to herself. "I want them to have the honor, to give the first push for the education of girls. If out of their slender purses they can do this, it'll be a great argument in raising the big sum later."

From house to house went Mary Lyon. She talked to mothers ambitious for their daughters. She talked to girls eager for a chance to study. She poured out her story in such a flood of happy explanation that listeners found no chance to stop her. Face to face with her they glimpsed a vision of the school through her radiant eyes.

"Invest a little corner of your farm or part of your town property in this seminary," she'd say. "What returns will it bring you? It'll put education within the reach of the common people."

"If you wanted a new shawl," she'd argue with the women, "or a table or a carpet, now wouldn't you find a way to get it?"

"Well, yes," they'd answer and give her ten dollars, or five, or fifty cents.

In two months she had the whole amount. Triumphant but tired out, Mary Lyon was pledged to the new school.

Now came the big task of securing the money for Mount Holyoke as the committee decided to call the seminary. Several ministers and professors traveled through the eastern states asking for pledges. But to Mary herself must go the credit for the largest part of these gifts. All her time she gave to getting subscriptions. Her own expenses she paid to the last penny.

All over New England she scurried by train and stage-coach. She was up at all hours. She was out in all weathers. She never stopped.

She talked in parlor meetings where well-to-do ladies were invited to hear her. She called on rich men in their offices and homes. In country churches, in district schoolhouses she offered people the chance to help. In the rumbling old stage-coach she'd outline her plan to the other travelers. Taking out her little green velvet bag she'd ask for gifts then and there.

On the road between Boston and Connecticut Mary Lyon and the green bag became a familiar sight.

" It's very bad taste," said her friends, " for you to journey about this way and beg for money."

But she protested, " My heart's sick of all your genteel nothingness! I'm doing a great work." And she'd add with a laugh, " I can't come down!"

Of course there were times when she was discouraged over her failure to interest people in the plan. But never once did

'ALL OVER NEW ENGLAND SHE SCURRIED BY STAGECOACH

she lose faith. Never did she harbor the idea of giving up the plan. She'd walk up and down the room and say over and over, " Commit thy way unto the Lord. He will keep thee.— Girls must be educated. They must be!"

At last her faith turned to hope. Slowly subscriptions came in. The three years' work was ended. There were two pledges of a thousand dollars each. There were many for a hundred. There were long lists of fives, twos and ones and fifty cents. There were three for six cents each.

Years later Mary Lyon used to show her girls several silver dollars that were blackened by fire. This was the story.

" Two spinsters promised us a hundred dollars each for Mount Holyoke. Soon after they lost their property in a fire. But their pledges must be met. With their own aristocratic hands they earned the money. These silver dollars were saved from the smoking embers of their home. But to me they seemed so precious that I replaced them with others and kept them so that Holyoke should always remember those faithful, old-maid sisters."

With such gifts of self-sacrifice, from the poverty of the common people the school was built.

When Harvard was two hundred years old the corner-stone of this seminary for girls was laid in the town of South Hadley in the Massachusetts hills. Stooping down Mary Lyon wrote on the stone, " The Lord hath remembered our low estate." You know that phrase in the Magnificat?

The cellar was nearly dug when quicksand was discovered.

The building had to be moved back some distance. Once started the walls fell in.

"Wasn't it fortunate," was Mary's way of meeting this calamity, "the masons were all at breakfast, so no one was hurt. Now when we rebuild the walls must be strengthened."

With thankful heart and busy hands she watched carpenters and painters at their work. She arranged for teachers and apparatus. She answered applications from three hundred girls. Shelves and closets, doors and sinks, tables and cupboards, she attended to every detail. With such care had she planned the building that very few changes were needed. And her success with all these practical things was the best answer to people who insisted, "Education will unfit a woman for every-day life."

The men had built the school. For the furnishing Mary Lyon turned to the women. Forty towns were asked each to do a room costing fifty or sixty dollars. The teachers and pupils in a near-by school gave money for a parlor. A gentleman furnished one room in memory of his daughter. A lady gave most of the china. There were gifts from children, from students, girls at home, from rich women and poor women—all Mary Lyon put to use.

Finally came the eighth of November, 1837. Stage-coaches and private carriages drove up to the five-storied brick building. The eighty chosen girls climbed down, and among them was your great-grandmother. Through the confusion they stumbled around to the side door.

A trustee was painting the steps at the entrance. Another tacked down matting. A third unloaded furniture. In the parlors were paint pots and work benches. Wives of trustees were washing dishes and peeling potatoes, setting up beds and putting chairs in place.

In the dining-room Miss Lyon greeted the newcomers.

"Unpack quickly," she said. "Roll up your sleeves and help put things in order."

On the stairs, in the kitchen, in the yard she gave the girls their entrance examinations. At four o'clock a bell rang. Trustees, teachers, students, all met in seminary hall. Mount Holyoke was opened.

The dream had come true. Mary Lyon had her school. It was endowed so that a year's tuition and board cost only sixty-four dollars. It had earnest, middle-class girls for pupils. Could this combination succeed?

From the very beginning her pet scheme about the house-keeping ran smoothly. With older girls for leaders the pupils cooked and swept, set the table and washed the dishes, dusted and ironed. All the work ran on a schedule. Many hands made light tasks. The hour a day of service was later cut in half. Holyoke was a constant lesson in system, in promptness and economy.

If Mary Lyon was a busy woman before now she never rested. For her enormous family she made a time-table which planned for study hours, for recitations and housework. She watched over classes and taught chemistry. She advised girls about choosing their subjects.   She ordered ink for the school-rooms, flour and potatoes for the kitchen, wood for the bed-rooms, and whale oil for the parlor lamps.   She made changes in her course of study and tried experiments.   She wrote out menus and supervised mending the linen.   She looked after homesick girls.   She took over the work of a sick teacher or a cook who married and left suddenly.   She watched the bread-making while she wrote the seminary letters.   Gently she sent away a girl who made mischief and wouldn't study.

Always she impressed on those first pupils that everything depended on them.

" Holyoke's an experiment in the eyes of the world," she'd warn them.   " The least act of any one of you will tell on its future and on the education of girls everywhere."

Thus she put on their shoulders a full share of responsi-bility.

At the end of the year there were two days of oral examina-tions to show what her pupils had accomplished.   A speaker from England was to address the graduates.   After he'd listened to questions and answers he gave up dinner and sleep to write a new speech.

" It would never do," he explained, " to present the simple one I brought with me."

Mary Lyon's plan had succeeded.   Joyfully she repeated the words of that other Mary, " My soul doth magnify the Lord."

What would the public say?   Would they stand loyally behind Mount Holyoke and send their daughters? Or would they desert it and let it be sold for a private academy? Four hundred girls more than could be accepted applied for the second year. That made the future sure and certain.

For twelve years Mary Lyon remained the principal. Without stint she gave herself to Holyoke. Her salary was two hundred dollars a year and she would accept no more. Hard as she had worked to start the seminary, she now worked to upbuild it. Her own beautiful character she stamped on school and pupils alike.

"For all her keen intellect," your great-grandmother used to describe her, " Miss Lyon had the warmest heart. To know her was in itself an education, we all felt. She wasn't strong-minded and cold, but sweet and lovable. And her face was like a benediction."

Yes, out of her own life she built Mount Holyoke. You can use your powers of invention to piece out slender funds, but it takes all your energy. In the end she paid the price. After a short illness Mary Lyon died at fifty-two when her friends thought she'd have fifteen or twenty years more to serve her school.

Under a great oak tree near the orchard they buried her, in the very heart of Holyoke. And on her monument is written a sentence from one of her last talks to the girls:

"There is nothing in the universe I fear, but that I shall not know all my duty or shall fail to do it."

To-day the busy college life flows around the spot. Near it pass the feet of girls whom she loved.

This Mary was just as much a pioneer as her sturdy ancestors who helped settle Massachusetts and built the old farmhouse where she was born. The education of girls began with her school. But it didn't stop there. How can we count up all the results of her work?

Steadily Mount Holyoke went on from seminary to college. The grounds were added to and made beautiful with trees and shrubbery. All the buildings of a modern college—gymnasium and library, art gallery, laboratories and dormitories—were built. The endowments were increased—far different from the days when fifty-cent subscriptions were gladly accepted! More than eight thousand girls have been educated there. All over the world they have spread Mary Lyon's ideal of service.

And you mustn't measure her work by Holyoke only. Wherever you go to college you'll be in debt to this Mary. To Wellesley? One of the Mount Holyoke trustees founded that college and two of its presidents were Mary Lyon's pupils. To Smith? The first president of the trustees of Smith served on the board at Holyoke. To Vassar? One of her students was its first lady principal. Many a boarding-school and high school with her pupils as teachers, owes its success to the training which she gave them. To one of the state universities? Opening their doors to women is one of the results of her work.

So this Mary made more time not by turning back the hour-glass, but by doubling and enriching her own life and the lives of girls everywhere.

THE MARY WITH A MAN'S NAME

Mary Ann Evans (George Eliot): 1819–1880

DO you see that row of books on the second shelf next the window, marked "The Works of George Eliot"? I suppose you've always thought they were some man's novels. Right next to them is the set of Charles Dickens. Then come Scott and Thackeray. Why shouldn't George Eliot be a man? But these are really a Mary's books. And the Mary Ann Evans who wrote them is, I believe, the most famous woman in English literature.

Why didn't she use her own name then? When she began to write she was very doubtful about succeeding. Her first story was printed in a magazine with no name at all. But her readers were curious. They insisted on finding out who the new author was. A name was necessary. So she chose George because her best friend was called that.

"And Eliot," said she, "because it's a good, mouth-filling

word, easy to pronounce. Then if George Eliot turns out to be a dull dog and this story's a mere flash in the pan, I'm determined to cut him!"

But tell you more about Mary Ann herself? She was an old-fashioned little girl like her name. She had long hair that hung over her eyes. She had pale cheeks like turnips. She was queer and not in the least pretty. And she was always in trouble, always being scolded about her clothes or her manners or her bad habit of reading in bed and wasting the candles.

Her sister Chrissey who was prim and neat and tidy, just the opposite of her, was the pet of all the aunts. Her brother was the mother's favorite and Mary the father's. They lived in the country, real English country. It had green fields and hedgerows and orchards. It had red-roofed cottages and sunny gardens. There were fine old trees that once upon a time made part of the famous and romantic forest of Arden.

Mr. Evans was the manager of a great estate. Very often he took Mary Ann with him as he drove about to see tenants and squires. The people they met were farmers and their wives, country parsons and village school teachers and doctors and little-town folks. She knew them all by heart.

For miles and miles together they drove through the quiet English landscape, the little wench, as her father called her, standing between his knees in the gig. Like a dry sponge the child soaked up this atmosphere. She absorbed it all so that she used to say years later, "Those scenes grew into my life."

And without half trying to remember she could repeat every word of talk she'd heard, or describe every detail of some happening.

An unusual child this Mary was. Everyone thought so. When she was only four years old she climbed up to the piano and played away though she didn't know one note from another.

"Why did you do that?" asked her father.

"To show one of the maids that I'm somebody," was her quaint reply.

She was seven when Chrissey borrowed a copy of Scott's *Waverly* and by some mischance returned it before the little sister was half through the story. How distressed she was! She began to write out the rest of the tale. The family were amazed. Her father sent for the book so she could read it to the end.

Though she wasn't often actually sick she was never very well. And I think she wasn't very happy either. Not when she was a child at home, playing with her brother. Not when she was at boarding-school where in all her classes she was far ahead of girls of her own age. They felt how superior she was and held aloof from her. Not one intimate friend did Mary have among them all.

Yet she longed for love and sympathy. She knew she was meant to be somebody in the world. She was always reaching out for something, she didn't know what. She despaired of ever accomplishing anything worth while. What she needed was encouragement from just the right person. What she lacked was belief in herself.

The years went by till the unhappy, restless Mary was thirty-seven. What was she doing all that time? She left school at fifteen. She devoted herself to her father. She played on the piano, she read aloud by the hour. About the housekeeping she was painstaking and conscientious. She made currant jelly and mince pies. She made damson cheese and butter. Years later when Londoners spoke of her beautiful hands she'd put them together and say, " See! the right hand is larger—that's because I used it so much in the dairy!"

And all this time she studied—French and German and Italian, as well as Greek and Latin. "With a dose of mathematics every day," she said, "to keep my brain from getting soft." She translated a German book into English, and very hard German it was. For a serious, sober magazine she wrote some serious, sober essays.

Then she met George Henry Lewes who was a writer himself. He discovered the wonderful gift that she had.

"I think you could write a capital story," he said. "You have wit and description—those two things go a good way toward making a novel. It's an experiment, of course. But it's worth trying."

Now for years Mary had had a vague dream of writing a novel. She'd done one chapter describing an English village. This she read aloud to Lewes.

"You must write," was his comment. "It may be a total

failure. Or it may be just good enough to warrant your trying again. Or you may do a masterpiece at once. There's no telling. But write you must!"

So she began a story. It wasn't one she invented, but about a poor minister's wife who was her mother's friend when she herself was a little girl. This was a new kind of novel. For it had no plot. It had no lovemaking. It had no happy marriage. It had no thrilling adventures. It was just a sketch of commonplace people that roused a reader's sympathy.

"Can you write good dialogue?" questioned Lewes. "I wonder how well you can manage a pathetic incident. Can you make the story dramatic?" Yet all the time he encouraged her.

One evening she read to him the chapter where good Mrs. Hackit leads the minister away from the bedside of poor Milly Barton. They both cried over it, just as I did and as I suppose you will. And Lewes kissed her as he said, "Your pathos is better than your fun."

A second and then a third story with ministers as the chief characters, followed *Amos Barton*. They were published in the magazine and then in book form. You see that one at the end of the shelf, *Scenes from Clerical Life?* And then she wrote a fourth, so long that *Adam Bede* makes a whole volume.

A great reputation George Eliot made for herself—or should I say for himself? Her closest friends didn't surmise that she was the author. Dickens was the only writer who guessed the new novelist to be a woman. Mrs. Carlyle thought he wasn't just a clergyman, but a minister's brother or cousin perhaps, with a wife who supplied all the little feminine touches. But when people in the neighborhood where the Evans family had lived read the first story they looked at each other excited and puzzled.

"Who wrote this?" they asked. "It must be someone who lives here. No one else could describe our church with the stone tower and the red baize doors and the iron pillars under the galleries. And how could anyone know the story of our minister's wife?"

They were only the more puzzled when the second sketch was printed, for it began with a conversation in the Red Lion Inn that many of them remembered word for word. It was a bit of talk Mr. Evans, I suppose, repeated to his wife. In her marvelous memory his little wench had stored it away.

When your grandmother and I were driving through the George Eliot country they showed us copies of this book. Written in the margins were the real names of the characters, fifty of them, and of a dozen places in the neighborhood. Years before Mary Ann Evans had been a schoolgirl there. Why connect her with *Amos Barton?*

Now there was in the town a solemn-faced preacher who was always about to do something. The village chose him as George Eliot.

"Did you," they asked pointblank, "write this book?"

He looked wise and smiled knowingly.

"Did you receive a large sum of money for it?"

" No."

And as he was very poor and did his own housework some well-meaning folks got up a subscription for him. To prevent fraud the secret had to be told. George Eliot was Mary Ann Evans!

Even her publisher had been kept in the dark. Lewes did all the corresponding and sent the manuscripts in, he said, for a friend. But just before the announcement was made he invited Blackwood to dinner to meet his new author. No Mr. Eliot appeared. There was only Miss Evans who acted as hostess and carved the roast. The three had a pleasant evening.

" I'm sorry," said the guest on leaving, " that George Eliot didn't come."

" Here he is," answered Lewes and turned to the lady across the room.

This first long story, *Adam Bede,* made a sudden leap into fame. Blackwood read through the first page of the manuscript. Then he put the roll into his pocket and said with a smile, " This'll do! "

Ministers and college professors, people who never read novels, all read this. One of its quaint sayings was quoted in Parliament. Critics praised it as the finest thing since Shakespeare. And this Mary said, " I sing my Magnificat in a quiet way and have a great deal of deep, silent joy."

She began her writing, you see, when she was middle-aged. She worked under great physical drawbacks. She had whole weeks of headaches, frequent sore throats and colds and attacks of rheumatism. Yet in twenty years she accomplished enough for the lifetime of most men.

With all her writing she was a first-rate housekeeper and a fine needlewoman. She used to say, " I've no patience with women who insist they must be excused from every-day duties because they can do something else well."

Of course publishers made her flattering offers that would have made her fortune. But she never dashed off three novels all alike.

" Good pay and bad writing," she explained, " don't tempt me."

I wish I could tell you how conscientious she was. She never wrote mechanically. She never wrote careless, slipshod paragraphs. When you look at her manuscripts you'll be surprised to see her exquisite, clear handwriting with scarcely a change or a word erased.

She spared no pains to make her work true. When she wanted the legal facts for Felix Holt to inherit an estate she consulted a lawyer. She pored over old Italian books to get the feel of Florence four hundred years ago. She spent long hours correcting proof sheets. She'd change the spelling of a word in dialect. She'd suggest what color a new volume should be.

What are her novels about? Are they all English stories? All but one. They're picture after picture of English life. They're rather somber, it's true, but brightened up with many a humorous touch. The very finest writing is about the people and things she knew best—her conscientious father, her mother who was sharp-tongued but tender-hearted, her relatives, the village people, the English country that had grown into her life. All these she put right into her books transforming them by her sympathy and imagination.

It doesn't make any difference whether she tells about Maggie's aunts with all their quaintnesses and their old-fashioned twists and ways, or about the glib, meddling rector's wife at Middlemarch, or the headstrong, violent miller on the Floss, or pretty Hetty making butter in the dairy—you have always the feeling that you've met these people and talked with them. You know how some portraits make you feel you can put your arm around the figure, so real it is? Every character is like that.

And what a memory this Mary had! Once her aunt who was a Methodist preacher, told her of spending a night in prison with a young woman who was to die the next morning. Years later at Lewes's suggestion she used this as the climax of Hetty's story in *Adam Bede*. One of the books has a description of an election riot. That she saw in her boarding-school days.

When she was a very little girl she met at twilight a linen weaver with a bag on his back. The picture stayed in her mind. Around it she wove the most beautiful perhaps of her novels. It's the one you are to read first of all. Why, yes, you may read it now.

Tell you a bit about it? It's the story of a forlorn, lonely, miserly weaver who loses his pile of gold pieces. He finds in its place, just the opposite of Midas, the curly, golden hair of a little child. He saves her from snow and death. And she in turn saves him and brings him into happy life with his fellows again. Which book is that? *Silas Marner.*

What are the rest about? One's the story of a brother and sister who are devoted to each other. Then pride and passion and sorrow part them. And the river Floss that made the background of their lives brings them together at last.

Maggie and Tom Tulliver are Mary Ann Evans and her brother. The prim, little pink-and-white cousin afraid of soiling her pinafore is Chrissey, the older sister. The books Maggie pored over, the gypsy adventure, the fishing, the attic, the round pool and the red deeps, all these are vivid memories from Mary's own childhood. *The Mill on the Floss*, at least Maggie Tulliver's early years, is half her own story.

Romola? That's about a man who loved pleasure and dreaded pain. And this weakness led Tito into falsehood and then little by little into crime against Romola and the city of Florence. Savonarola, the famous reformer-monk, is one of the people in this book. It's your grandmother's favorite. And it was Mary Ann Evans' favorite too. Some of the critics say *Romola* is her very best work. More than that, they say it's the greatest historical novel ever written.

What a world of pleasure you have ahead of you getting acquainted with all George Eliot's people! How I envy you reading these books for the first time! There are so many things you'll like—the beautiful English where she seems to have always just the right word, and the little preachments where she leaves the story to talk to her readers, and the exquisite paragraphs about music where her people sing or play or listen with the keen pleasure she herself felt. Did I tell you she was born on St. Cecilia's day and always called herself Cecilia's child?

And running through all these novels like a thread of gold is the lesson she had in mind—to teach men to be more tender to each other's suffering, more fair to each other's faults. The more you know of this Mary's books the more you'll want to know about her own life, to see how much of herself she put into her characters. So you'll want to read her letters and journal.

You'll feel then as though you'd been to one of her Sunday afternoon receptions where the most famous literary and scientific people of London were her guests. There at the end of the room near the fire, dressed in black velvet with a lace scarf over her head, she sits in a low chair bending forward a little as she talks.

Like a magnet she draws friends about her. Some admire her because she's a fine musician. Some come to the house because she's a deep thinker, master of many languages and many sciences. Still others like her because she's sweet and tender, a woman of great dignity and earnest character.

Or perhaps you may be one of the more intimate group spending the evening in her drawing-room. She'll play Bee-

SHE'LL PLAY BEETHOVEN ON THE NEW PIANO

thoven on the new grand piano. Tennyson will read some of his poems. Browning comes to tell her that a bust of Savonarola has just been found in Florence. And the visitors look at the picture of Romola's friend and then at George Eliot and say, "How alike their faces are!"

The English that Mary Ann Evans wrote is simple. Her characters are fresh and varied. They're just stupid, everyday people who are picturesque and tragic when touched by her sympathy. A deep, rich humor she had. Like Shakespeare she could borrow the idea for a story and make it into a dramatic, gripping tale.

Through all these years her novels have been read more and more. They're not limited to any one country or to any one time. For the struggle between good and evil, questions of duty and conscience, are problems of the human heart everywhere and always.

This Mary is, I told you, our greatest woman writer. Do you see now why we keep her books just above the set of Dickens and side by side with Thackeray and Scott? Which of these novelists are men, which women makes no difference. They belong together at the very head of the list in English literature. And this place of honor Mary won though she didn't begin to write till she was nearly forty. Oh, how you'll enjoy knowing her books and her!

FALL INTO LINE!

Mary A. Livermore: 1821-1905

"SH! SH! Come here. Sh!"

Mr. Rice put his finger on his lips and motioned for his wife to follow him. Across the kitchen he went and down the back steps, through the yard toward the woodshed. Wondering she hurried along close behind him. Suddenly she heard the voice of her little daughter.

" Let us sing hymn five hundred and forty-one."

Ah, now she knew. The children were playing church again.

The mother and father tiptoed up to a window. Mary's back was toward them. The children facing her were intent on their hymn-books. Unnoticed the parents watched a moment, then stepped back to listen.

In the woodshed were a dozen boys and girls of the neighborhood and Mary's little sisters. Great logs were laid out for pews. To eke out the congregation sticks of wood were set up on them. What a leader Mary was, choirmaster and minister all in one, singing, praying, preaching. Her mother smiled at her earnestness.

"Oh," said her father soberly, "if Mary'd been a boy we'd have trained her for the ministry."

Preachers in plenty there'd been among her Welsh ancestors —six generations of them. Her parents were strict Calvinists and brought up their children as strictly. Serious and earnest, ten-year-old Mary felt herself responsible for the conversion of her little sisters. Sometimes at night she could not sleep for worrying about them. She'd slip out of bed and waken her mother, begging her to pray for them.

"But what about you, child?"

"No matter about me," she answered, "if they can be saved I can bear anything."

In public school in Boston Mary was quick to learn. She was a great favorite with all the teachers because she was so enthusiastic over her work, with the girls and boys because she was a born leader. Especially did poor, unfortunate children love her. Eagerly she championed a lad in shabby clothes or a little girl with scanty lunch. They would walk home with her, because her mere presence was a sign of "hands off" to the biggest bully of that neighborhood.

With all this she was no prig, but a merry, wholesome child. She was fond of all kinds of outdoor sport. Sliding on the ice was her special delight. After an hour's fun in the cold, bracing air she rushed into the house one winter afternoon exclaiming, " Splendid! the sliding's splendid! "

" Yes, splendid! " replied her father. " It's good fun, Mary, but hard on shoes."

Instantly her rosy face sobered. Six children—one father who worked very hard—shoes, shoes that wore out constantly. Was her sliding on the ice adding to the family burdens? She'd never slide again. And she did not.

When she was eleven she decided she must earn money herself. She hated sewing, but that seemed the one trade possible for her to take up. After three months as an apprentice she was hired in a dressmaking shop for thirty-seven cents a day. Such a wage would never meet her ambitions. So she asked for work at a clothing store.

" I'll give you a dozen red flannel shirts to make," said the man. " I want them just as soon as possible, for business is rushing now. Six and a quarter cents apiece." He took down her name and address and handed her the bundle.

Mary took it to her own room without saying a word about her plan. Every night she sewed for hours. But it was slow work. She could not finish those twelve red shirts on time.

" Does Mary Rice live here? " a strange man asked when Mrs. Rice answered a ring at the bell.

" Yes."

" Well, she took a dozen shirts from my shop. Why hasn't she returned them? "

"You must be mistaken, sir. It can't be my daughter."

"Mary Ashton Rice—Salem Street." The man looked at the card in his hand and glanced up at the Old North Church, four doors away, to prove that he was right.

"Yes, Mother," Mary's voice interrupted at that moment, "I did get the shirts from this man."

"And you promised, miss, to get them made. I'm in a very great hurry for them."

"You shall have them all to-morrow night," answered the girl.

"Very well."

Mrs. Rice burst into tears. "Oh, Mary, Mary, we're not so poor as that. What will become of my little daughter if she takes all the cares of the world upon her shoulders?"

The two sat down together to work on those flannel shirts and succeeded in finishing them by the next evening. When the seventy-five cents was paid her Mary took only half, insisting that this was all she'd earned.

All her spare time she read or studied. At school she won a medal for good scholarship. Friends of the family insisted that her education must go further and arranged for her to attend the Charlestown Seminary. Before her first term ended one of the teachers died and Mary was asked to take her place. This work paid her tuition and she found time to keep on studying, and recited out of hours.

Latin and French she taught and her pupils liked her. They were too much interested in her method to think how very young she was. Indeed she seemed far older than she really was because of her quiet, womanly ways.

Then came two years in Virginia where she taught a private school for the children of a great plantation. Pleasant months those were. But her real reason for going into a southern state was to see for herself what slavery was. Were Lucretia Mott and Whittier right in all they said against it? On that Virginia plantation were five hundred negroes. She lived face to face with the best and the worst of slavery. She went back to Massachusetts with strong feelings against it and a longing to see it abolished.

At twenty she was in charge of a high school in Duxbury. Touched by her enthusiasm and magnetism even the dullest boys and girls learned. Soon hers became a model high school. But she could remain its principal for only three years.

On Christmas Eve she was taking a walk. Attracted by the music she went into a church near the school. Her younger sister had died and Mary was in great sorrow. As if he had known her special need the minister preached a sermon full of comfort. To his surprise Miss Rice asked to take it home to read it again.

When she returned the sheets of that sermon she borrowed some books. To his further surprise he found that while she was interested in his talks and his library, he was becoming interested in her. You can guess the sequel. The Mary Rice who used to preach to sticks of wood in the shed became Mrs.

Daniel Parker Livermore, the wife of the young minister in Duxbury.

In Connecticut and Massachusetts, in western New York the Livermores lived as the husband accepted one pastorate after another. A busy time this was for his wife, for she was always the leader. She helped in every kind of church work. She edited a paper for children. She wrote sketches and stories for magazines. She started reading clubs among the young people and a current events class for Saturday nights. She worked in many charities. She served on committees and boards.

In 1857 the Livermores were living in Chicago. The husband was editor of a church paper. Mary was his assistant, often left in charge of printing office and the staff of workers. She went on writing for eastern publications. In addition she kept house, directed the servants, watched over the education and training of the three children. All ordinary, every-day duties, she'd have said. No woman ever became famous for doing them well.

But in Illinois, in the nation great events were about to take place. Step by step the question of slavery had become the most vital matter of the day. From her quiet, sheltered home in Chicago, with its daily cares and work and all its happiness Mary Livermore looked out on a land over which dark clouds of war were gathering.

She witnessed the stir and excitement at first hand. In May of 1860 she sat at the press table in the "Wigwam," the only woman reporter among more than a hundred men. She heard the cheering when the names of Seward and Lincoln were placed before the Republican convention. She kept tally as the roll was called, as states changed their votes and "the rail splitter" was nominated for the presidency.

In the early spring of the next year Mary Livermore was summoned to Boston. Her father was very ill. The day after her arrival Fort Sumter was fired on. New England was indignant and excited. From sickroom to the bulletin-board Mary passed back and forth taking the latest news to Mr. Rice.

When he heard that Sumter had fallen he turned his face to the wall with a bitter cry. "Now let me die. I cannot survive the ruin of my country." The son of a Revolutionary soldier, impressed by the British, escaping to take a part in the war of 1812, he was enthusiastic in his love for the republic. Its heroism and its glory were burned into him in boyhood as they were burned into his daughter Mary.

Lincoln called for volunteers. Mr. Rice rallied when he heard the North's answer—four or five men offering for every man who could be accepted. When troops began arriving in Boston he insisted on being lifted into a carriage to witness their reception. Oh, the cheering from ten thousand people as the stars and stripes floated out over Faneuil Hall!

Mary Livermore knew the full measure of slavery. Though she'd lived almost all her life in New England she never dreamed its citizens could be so fired with a warlike spirit. She was in the enormous crowd at the station when the first Massachusetts regiment left for Washington. What shouts as the thousand men marched in! A hush fell on the excited people.

"Fall into line!"

At the unfamiliar words the boys in their new blue coats slipped from the clinging arms of mothers and wives and sweethearts. Company by company they marched into the long train. The engine whistled good-bye. From the crowd sounded a roar of good wishes and parting words.

Fall into line! Who would command the women of the North?

This picture of excitement and patriotism Mary Livermore described to her aged father. It was like a tonic giving him a new lease of life. He became much better. She could return to Chicago.

Her husband had written her of the war fever there. Boston, she found, was calmness itself in comparison with the prairie city. Everywhere there were stir and excitement. The streets were thronged with eager men and women engrossed by the war news, the war spirit, the war preparations.

The scene in the Boston station Mary Livermore saw repeated when the first Illinois troops started south. Thousands of people were cheering. Shrill whistles along the lake shore bade the train Godspeed.

"I have no son to send," she said to herself. "What can women do?"

What can women do? All through the North women were asking that same question. The men had answered Lincoln's call without regard to politics or party, to trade or creed. The women were just as loyal, just as devoted. What to do? What to make? Where to send?

It was the beginning of summer. The soldiers were going south. A newspaper printed an account of General Havelock who devised a white linen head-dress for his soldiers to wear over their caps to protect them from sunstroke in India. Havelocks! ordered some inexperienced men in the army. Havelocks, havelocks! answered the inexperienced women.

Eagerly they set to work. Through the Middle West raged a havelock furor. Women made them in all-day meetings. They were cut out and sent to homes to be stitched. Day and night sewing machines ran till the nondescript white head-gear was finished. Havelocks were turned in at central stations— havelocks of all patterns and sizes, havelocks of every possible material, havelocks for squads, for companies, for regiments.

With a committee of ladies Mary Livermore went out to Camp Douglas near Chicago. The nineteenth Illinois received them. Out from the rows of tents came the boys, all wearing that ugly white head-dress. There were havelocks made into nightcaps and turbans. There were havelocks worn as bandages and sunbonnets. In every imaginable fashion those young soldiers carried them.

Officers of the regiment and committee of ladies shouted at the ludicrous sight. They laughed till they cried. Havelocks went out of style. What could soldiers do with them? So much wasted labor and energy, the work of busy hands and warm hearts! What could the women do?

There came a mania for lint and bandages. That was the one topic of conversation. What's the best material for lint? How do you scrape it? How can it be gathered in the largest quantities? How do you roll this bandage? All over the city of Chicago the eager women opened lint and bandage stations. Every household was scraping and rolling. Then a machine was put to work making lint.

Fall into line! What to do?

East and west, in town and village, earnest and patriotic women were all asking that question. In one Connecticut city they organized for some vague service on the very day of the president's call for volunteers. By the end of April there were many relief societies in existence. Zeal and eagerness there were aplenty. But no one gave them direction or guidance.

As soon as the men were mustered into the army and marched away to fife and drum, the women of each neighborhood would take steps to provide home comforts for the well, hospital supplies and nursing for the sick and wounded. It was an admirable plan—on paper. The one trouble was that it couldn't be carried out.

Boxes and packages addressed to the soldiers were lost. They could not be delivered because regiments moved about constantly, because a colonel or captain in whose care they were sent had been transferred. In express and freight offices perishable goods accumulated until officials were in despair. Broken jars and jelly glasses, decaying fruit and vegetables, sweet-meats that were fermenting spoiled the blankets and clothing in which they were wrapped. The lavish giving of the North meant an equally lavish waste and loss.

Out of this chaos of individual generosity and neighborhood patriotism came the Sanitary Commission. The fifth wheel of the coach, officers in the war department called it at the start, but shortly changed their minds. It offered carefully made plans for collecting and distributing supplies and funds. It provided a marvelous system not for the men of one particular neighborhood or regiment, nor from a certain state, but for any soldiers who were in need.

People were suspicious of the Commission. Only by experience did the North learn how far-seeing were its plans, how efficient its methods. Gradually it gained the confidence of the public, gained too in scope. It became the one channel through which gifts flowed to the army.

Hard work Mary A. Livermore had to persuade the aid society in her neighborhood to enlist under the Sanitary Commission, to follow its directions about supplies, to give their money through its treasury. For a year a dozen or more organizations of Chicago women worked on independently, interested in helping the soldiers whom they personally knew.

When her own aid society joined with the Commission Mrs. Livermore began giving it more and more of her time and energy. Soon she was appointed its agent not for Chicago only, not for Illinois only, but for the six states then termed the

North West. She was the general for the women of Illinois and Indiana, Wisconsin and Michigan, Iowa, Minnesota, grouped in nearly four thousand aid societies. Count them with only ten members each, they were an army of forty thousand.

Fall into line! Mary A. Livermore had the truest patriotism plus fine executive ability. She had a physical strength to match her active brain. Her great power as a leader, her interest in young people, her housewifely instincts, her sympathy with the unfortunate, her zeal in taking burdens upon her own shoulders—all this was now to be used in the service of the nation. What could women do? She was ready to tell them.

Much of her work at first was organizing aid societies. In a country schoolhouse, in a church at the crossroads, in some central farmhouse of a scattered community, in village, town, city she would call a group of women together and talk with them. She told them how to start, what materials to buy, what to make, how to cut and sew, how to pack and list and ship, where to send, what to do with money, with hospital supplies, with food. No more havelocks! No more lint scraping! No more wasted energy!

Over and over she answered the same question as she journeyed through her six states visiting her aid societies: " But why doesn't the government do this? "

" The government," she would say, " has all it can do—and more. It's taxed to the utmost to provide food and arms and shelter for the fighting men. You know how gigantic our armies are, now that we've learned this war isn't a matter of three months. As for the sick ——"

And she'd go on to explain something of military hospitals and commissaries; how, to prevent waste and loss, regulations were necessary, fixed rations and supply tables; how amounts of food and medicines were based on the average number of sick men; how difficult it was to adjust peace rules for a small army or a little Indian war to such needs as a great emergency might bring at any moment.

" Our boys may need more than the ordinary rations if there's lots of sickness where a camp's in an unhealthy locality; if a battle has been fought—and battles come at unexpected times, in unexpected places. The government has no way to meet these emergencies. The Sanitary Commission has. It will meet them if we give it supplies enough and money enough. It has only one rule: Have supplies enough so that the last are never used.

" You ask me if the gifts you send really reach the soldiers? Is there any truth in the stories floating about, of doctors and nurses feasting on delicacies addressed to their patients? At first there may have been some waste, some thieving, but it was the exception, not the rule. And there's none now—not now. This is how the Commission keeps account of your boxes of bandages, your cans of fruit and preserves."

Then she'd tell the listening group how she started her children off to school each morning and rode on the street-car to the Sanitary Commission's rooms on Madison Street—under

McVicker's theater; how she always found several drays backed
up to the curb and the sidewalks piled high with boxes and bales
and parcels; how John, the man-of-all-work, registered and
opened them, checked up the precious contents by the list nailed
inside the cover; how her helpers sorted them, stamped each
article "Chicago Sanitary Commission" and repacked all of
one kind in a box, for the convenience of the hospitals; how
they were shipped to storage station or division hospital as the
latest orders directed; and how finally vouchers signed by head
surgeons or head nurses came back to the North West headquarters.

"Precious contents I said about the boxes your aid society
sends in. Precious is often not a strong enough adjective to
describe them. When we begged for blankets they came in
quantity, new blankets that had never been used, old and
threadworn blankets that represented a real sacrifice on the
part of some boy's mother. Such pitiful and touching notes as
come in these packages: from a young wife whose husband lost
his life at Shiloh; from a group of little girls who used their
own money to buy some materials and made all the garments in
their box and wrote a dear letter to the soldiers who were to
wear them in some hospital; from the lady of eighty-six who
knit so many pairs of socks;" then with a quick change as she
saw tears on the faces of the women in front of her, "Sometimes tacked on the inside of the lid, along with the list, I find
a solemn warning: 'Surgeons and Nurses, HANDS OFF! These
things are for your patients!' And once we opened a box to

find a bushel of cookies tied up in a pillow-case labeled, 'For sick soldiers. If anybody else eats them I hope they choke him!'

"But do supplies get to the place where they're needed, you ask. Last Thanksgiving in Tennessee one of the Sanitary agents was talking to the surgeon in charge of a division hospital. Up came an assistant with a long face. 'Doctor, what shall we do? Our supplies have not come. The wounded men are lying on the ground without even blankets. No dressings, no proper food. If only we could get in touch with the Sanitary Commission!' Without a word the surgeon turned to your agent. In an hour they were unloading bedding and dressings, milk and concentrated beef, hospital clothes and fresh vegetables. 'Bless the Sanitary!' exclaimed the doctors together."

To another group of women asking the old question she would say, "I wonder if your village has a grumbler writing home? I suppose every regiment has one or two such men. Soldiering isn't easy at the best. Conditions aren't ideal—this is war. But sometimes great harm is done by the chronic grumblers who write such gloomy, discouraging letters. The stewards get half the things you send, the poor soldiers nobody considers? Yes, I've heard that over and over again.

"One doctor told me of such a croaker in his hospital. For a week he took away from the man everything which had been given by the Commission—his pocket comb, his handkerchief, his slippers and dressing gown, his looking-glass, his feather pillow, his books. He slept on a hard, hair pillow under a government blanket. He had his meals at a separate table on commissary rations. He was cured!

"And we mustn't blame the men altogether. Sometimes they don't know who sends them milk and crutches, clean sheets and potatoes—oh, how hungry they all are for potatoes! In a ward of convalescents a friend of mine came across a soldier with a bandaged hand who asked him to address the envelope for a letter to his wife. 'She says up home the aid society's getting some Sanitary supplies ready and she's going to put in a nice lot of goods. I've told her not to do any such thing— we never get what is sent.' Several other men spoke up: 'That's so. Never see any Sanitary things here. Officers must feast on them, the common soldiers get none.' My friend turned to the man holding the letter. 'I'm sure you must be wrong. Where'd you get all these things?' pointing to pillow and socks, slippers and clean sheets, and to the trays just being brought in, with butter and tomatoes and pickles. 'I reckon Uncle Sam fitted up this hospital, he provides them in the linen room and the pantry.' 'They're not to be bought in the market here for love or money,' said the visitor. 'Let's call in the steward.' So the steward was sent for, and at his first words the men hung their heads in confusion. 'Why, boys, didn't you know you get all these things from the Sanitary Commission?' The man with the letter tore it into shreds. 'I'll write my wife another and tell her to go ahead with their supplies. Right glad we'll be to get them from the Sanitary.'"

Work enough for one woman this organizing of aid societies would seem to be. But Mary Livermore wrote and wrote and wrote during those four years of war. A story of her day's work in the Chicago office she would send to some Eastern magazine. Sketches of young soldiers, of a hospital ward, of women harvesting their wheat she would write for the newspapers or her husband's periodical. Three columns a week and often more she did. Each month she sent a bulletin to her aid societies. By reports and circulars and letters she kept in close touch with each group and so kept them all on the alert.

And the letters! Mothers wrote her for news of their boys. Dying soldiers begged her to write home for them. Wounded men wrote her about their furloughs, their children, their back pay or pensions. Every letter from a soldier or about a soldier she answered whether she'd ever known the man or not. After long hours in the office she would take home the day's mail and write far into the night. Her notes were like a flame that kindled the patriotism of women all through the North West.

Fall into line! What Mary A. Livermore and her aid societies could do in time of emergency! The army in Tennessee gave notice that the government wanted to buy fifty thousand bushels of potatoes and large quantities of other vegetables. To this appeal there was no response. Was there a real scarcity? Was transportation so difficult? Did farmers fear a rigid government inspection? No potatoes, no onions were offered. In despair officials turned to the Sanitary Commission.

Scurvy was threatening the troops in Tennessee! Scurvy, that dread of every army, the scourge that takes more lives than falling shells, the disease that can't be healed by medicines, that can be prevented in only one way—a diet with fresh vegetables. Scurvy!

Back went a telegram to those disheartened commissary officers: "Shipments of vegetables from Louisville already under way. Will be continued."

Out from the Chicago office went the appeal: Onions, potatoes, sour kraut—onions and potatoes to meet the threat of scurvy.

It was March, a rainy month in the states of the North West. Bad roads made transportation almost impossible. But in spite of mud and weather the women of the aid societies canvassed house by house, district by district, asking for potatoes and onions.

"The soldiers don't stop for weather. Why should we?"

People who could gave by the bushel. Families who could spare them gave pecks. Some gave only a quart. Some gave a handful. Thus the precious stores were collected, homely vegetables worth more than their weight in gold. The aid societies held special meetings to pack these strange supplies. They begged for barrels and kegs. The men cut up the cabbage, the women packed it with layers of salt and poured vinegar over the whole. Down the railroad, down the Mississippi went sour kraut and onions and potatoes, joining the homes in the North with Vicksburg by a chain of vegetables.

The usual boxes of supplies did not lessen. In addition a hundred barrels a day went from Chicago, sometimes a hundred and fifty. An anxious three weeks the Sanitary leaders had. An anxious time too for mothers and wives and sisters. What joyful news when the telegram came from Vicksburg: "Scurvy stamped out. The Sanitary Commission has saved the army!"

Sometimes Mrs. Livermore left the office for a few weeks to take a group of nurses to the front, to distribute a boatload of supplies, to make a tour of inspection. The Commission asked her to report on the hospitals in and near St. Louis, hastily established after the unconditional surrender of Fort Donelson. The next winter she went through camps and hospitals along the Mississippi and near Vicksburg.

She kept her eyes open. With a housewife's keen instinct for details she saw where improvements could be made. Her suggestions she made to army officers and medical directors, not to the public, not to the papers, not to the folks at home. On a second visit she would note all the changes and these facts she would tell and advertise widely.

This work she did so well that she helped build the reputation of the Sanitary Commission. She helped build too, through all the villages and towns of her six states, a national sentiment. She worked for the Union soldiers, not for boys from Michigan or Illinois; national, national, national, she said and wrote constantly, never local. How much this helped to stop unjust criticism of the government, to stop talk of an early peace

HER VISITS TO THE RIFLE PITS DID MUCH FOR THE MEN

during dark days of trouble and defeat, can never be known.
Women were helping to form public opinion.

Building thus for the Commission and for the federal government, she did as great a service for the women of the North.
Harder to wait at home than to be in the thick of the fight.
They had no time now to grieve, to lose heart. She put them
to work, at work she showed them to be needed. She kept
them at it week after week, month after month. Impossible to
work for the relief of the soldiers without faith in the triumph
of their cause! Fall into line! A certain amount of supplies
Mary Livermore set as the quota for each aid society. That
number must be sent in. Steady and persistent must be the
flow of supplies. Have enough on hand so that the last are
never used.

Her visits to posts along the Mississippi, to the rifle pits in
front of Vicksburg did far more than give her material to write
about or to tell the people at the North. How much they did
for the men! Everywhere she was a messenger of good tidings.
The sight of a woman's face, the sound of a woman's voice was
a touch of home to the boys in blue. She scattered her supplies
with cheering words. They forgot the hardness of their lot.

"Is that all for me?" asked one soldier to whom she gave a
little package of white sugar, tea and onions. He burst into
tears. "God bless the women up home!" he sobbed out. "I
came from father's farm. I've been sick here three months.
I've seen no lady till to-day and it unmans me. But don't
think I rue my bargain, I'd go through it all for the old flag."

"Why, lady, where'd you come from? Did you drop from heaven?" the boys asked when an officer took her into the rifle pits where the heat was stifling, where the Minié balls were whizzing.

"I've come from your friends at home. I bring you the comforts we owe you and love to give. I've come to see if you get what they send you."

"Do they think as much of us as all that? Why, boys, we can fight another year on that, can't we?"

"Yes, yes," they cried in chorus.

She shook hands all around and said good-bye.

"Mrs. Livermore," begged one officer, "promise you'll visit my regiment to-morrow. It'll be worth a victory to them. They'll talk of you for six months to come. You don't know what good a lady's visit to the army can do! Around the fires, in the rifle pits, in the dark night, on the march they'll repeat your words and describe your looks and voice and dress. On one thing they'll all agree—that you look like an angel, and exactly like each man's wife or mother."

Her gentleness and tender sympathy she poured out on sick and wounded men. Sick soldiers were always so much more disheartened than the wounded. Sent to inspect for the Commission Mary Livermore turned her hand to any service. She did errands, wrote letters, mended, and cooked.

At Young's Point she came across a group of sick boys waiting to be moved to St. Louis. There was no kitchen. There was nothing to cook in, no stove to cook on. But she had an alcohol lamp, a little teapot, a supply of alcohol.

"Boys," she said cheerily, "you'll soon be moved and I'll stay with you till that steamer comes for you. The folks at home sent me down here. They gave me everything you need. Just look!"

Before their eyes she made tea, sweetened it, and added some milk. "Tea, tea," they began calling out, "tea with white sugar and milk in it!" For three days she made tea for them over her alcohol lamp. She made them soup with extract of beef. She heard the story of their troubles. They were happier and more hopeful than had seemed possible in that forlorn spot. When the steamer finally arrived she saw them carried on board, given warm baths and fresh garments, and put into sweet, clean beds as they started up the river.

The government worked with men in quantity. To Mary Livermore every soldier was an individual. Each man was not a "case," but a boy to be helped. She was never too busy to look after this special soldier, to supply a little delicacy to that one. Here her woman's gift of detail proved a help.

From one church in Chicago thirty-four young men enlisted together. Among them was a clerk named Turner, a great favorite with everyone. He was frail and could not stand army hardships. He broke down and was sent to a St. Louis hospital. Friends begged for him to come home. But he could not be released, something was wrong with his papers. Influential relatives made trips to St. Louis, but poor Turner was held fast by the red-tape of army regulations. They appealed to Mrs. Livermore.

"If you men could accomplish nothing, what do you expect a woman can do?"

"Your tact and perseverance can overcome any obstacle. Pray go down to St. Louis."

She went and was told, as the others had been told, that Turner's descriptive list was missing. The hospital had written to his commanding officer. The battery was moving constantly. It might be months before the answer came. Turner said he had given his list to the doctor's clerk. It must be in this office somewhere, thought Mary A. Livermore.

The clerk's face flushed with annoyance, but he could not refuse to show her the lists for Ward D. One by one he turned them over and she read aloud the name endorsed on the back.

"Stop! Isn't that it?" she cried as she saw a familiar name.

"No. That's cheated all of Turner's friends. His name is Lowell D. Turner and this, you see, is Loring D. Turner."

"Open it, let's see the inside."

There was the name correctly written, but wrongly endorsed on the back. There was the missing list! The medical director wrote an order for Turner's discharge. Another stumbling block. Two weeks' papers were ahead of this one, asserted a pert little lieutenant, they must be done strictly in order unless General Curtis said one should receive immediate attention. No, she could not see General Curtis. He was holding a meeting with his staff officers.

What to do? It was past noon and the train left at three.

"My dear madam, what can I do for you?" An officer she knew came up to Mrs. Livermore in the hall.

"Get me five minutes with General Curtis and you'll make me the most grateful woman in St. Louis."

"Come with me."

Into that staff meeting she went, secured a written permission to take Turner north that afternoon and hurried back to Ward D. As she opened the door every soldier looked at her questioningly. Turner sitting up in bed gasped and was deadly white.

"Don't faint," she said. "You're going to Chicago with me this afternoon. Here is the order from General Curtis. Your papers and back pay will be sent you."

"Bully for you, Turner," called out the man in the next bed. The others crowded around rejoicing, cheering the general and Mrs. Livermore. Half a dozen soldiers who could be on their feet formed a mimic band with bugles, drums and bagpipes. Turner fainted from all the excitement. But he lived to reach his friends, and for ten years afterward.

On one of her river tours Mary Livermore discovered twenty-three sick and wounded soldiers left at a station with insufficient care. They had no chance to go home, for no one had authority to discharge them. A knot of red tape tied them down. At a glance she took in the situation. She went to Grant's headquarters. Without waiting to take the chair offered her she told her story in a few words.

"General, if you'll give me authority to do so, I'll take those twenty-three men safely home."

He eyed her in silence. So many women came down the Mississippi on errands more enthusiastic than practical. Mrs. Livermore was a stranger to him. Silently her eyes replied. Without a word to her he gave the necessary order. Soon she was on her way with her men.

For months it was hard to make people realize the Sanitary Commission's need of money. Twice as interesting to give bandages as to give a dollar. The more supplies were sent in, the more organization was needed to distribute them. The longer the war lasted, the more battles were fought, the more men there were to be helped, the more the Sanitary had to do. Money, money, money was needed.

Mary Livermore proposed a Sanitary Fair in Chicago, not for the city only, but for the six states working under that office of the Commission. They would raise ten thousand dollars, said the women. They made plans on a mammoth scale. They hired fourteen halls. They went into debt.

"Give up this fair," urged the men of the prairie city in alarm. "We'll give the Sanitary Commission twenty-five thousand dollars when we think it's needed."

"No," said the women quietly, "we'll hold our fair."

During three months of preparation there was no slackening of ordinary Sanitary work. A contribution from every person, said the women. Everyone can give something. Newspapers as well as business men opposed the fair and made sport of it.

"A potato parade" they called the great procession with which the first day was to start. Mary Livermore smiled and worked the harder.

For the opening of the Sanitary Fair the railroads ran excursion trains to Chicago. Bells rang. One hundred guns were fired. Children were dismissed from school. Heading the parade were wagons, driven by farmers' wives and daughters, filled with their gifts of onions and potatoes for which another army in the south was clamoring. The long line halted in the march past the Livermore house. The eyes of the spectators were blurred with tears.

The women sold articles of every kind—live stock and plows and reapers, trunks and sewing machines and stoves. They served dinners and gave concerts and tableaux. They had a curiosity shop and an art exhibit. When it was over they had made not ten, but a hundred thousand dollars.

Chicago set the fashion. In other cities Sanitary Fairs were held. The treasury was filled again and again. Entirely aside from the money, these fairs were important because they proved that interest in the soldiers' welfare had not lessened.

"Please come over to Dubuque," wrote a group of women to Mary A. Livermore, "and tell us how to plan a fair."

She went and found to her consternation that she was to address not the ladies of an aid society, but a great audience in the largest church in the city.

"I cannot," she answered when her hostess exclaimed that this was a splendid opportunity, the whole state would be listening. "I cannot. I've never spoken in public—just to little groups of women. I sit down with my hands in my lap and just talk. I can't deliver a real lecture. Oh, why did you plan all this without telling me?"

"How dare you say you can't," gently urged a colonel who had met her at the front, near battlefields, in hospital wards. "God has given you this chance to enlist the state of Iowa. How dare you refuse? Tell the people just what you'd have said to the aid society. But don't let this glorious opportunity end in failure!"

Mary Livermore could not say again, "I cannot." Instead she answered, "I will try. But be sure you tell them that I'm not a public speaker."

How frightened she was when she stepped out on that platform! The audience was like so many sticks of wood set up in the pews. Their faces blurred and ran together. She could not hear her own voice. Suddenly the scene before her was blotted out. She saw rows of white faces in hospital beds, faces of young boys of eighteen and twenty, faces stamped with suffering, with patience uncomplaining. She forgot her fears. She remembered only that Iowa's help was needed.

Spellbound that great audience listened for nearly two hours. Then faster than secretaries could take down names and amounts the gifts came in—eight thousand dollars in cash, bushels and bushels of potatoes and onions, barrels of sour kraut, hundreds of hospital suits. Then and there a committee for the Iowa fair was appointed and a great success it was.

That speech in Dubuque did more than rouse an entire state to work for the Sanitary Commission. It proved that Mary A. Livermore was an orator. Never again was she afraid to speak before a great audience. Her voice she used for the soldiers as well as busy hands and active brain.

And the war over, the emergency become routine again, she found that soldiers were needed for peace too. Other causes needed speakers. Mary A. Livermore fell into line once more. She became a public lecturer and for years traveled over the country, speaking in every state in the Union as well as in Europe and Canada. Five times a week for five months each year, her manager planned appointments for her. In the decade when the lyceum bureaus were at the height of their popularity she was one of the four speakers most in demand, one of the four best paid; the other three were men.

A lecture on the education of girls she gave no less than eight hundred times from Maine to California. She talked on her experiences in the war, on her days in the Sanitary Commission.

" Steer clear of temperance and suffrage," advised her manager, " and you'll be rich."

" No," was her answer. " Men need one and women the other. I'll give a temperance talk whenever I'm invited to. I'll speak for suffrage at every opportunity."

Constantly in these lecture trips war incidents kept coming up. Mothers showed her letters she had written for their boys. Wives brought her little keepsakes she had sent home for dying husbands. Children thanked her for what she'd done for their fathers. In hundreds of households she found that her name was known and remembered lovingly.

One day a six-foot man came up to her after a lecture.

" Do you remember coming over to a hospital east of Memphis? "

" Yes."

" Do you remember coming into one ward and saying we could all have a glass of milk with every meal? "

" I often did that."

" And one major cried and said he wanted two cups of milk. You patted him on the head as he lay on his cot. And thinking of his home folks whom he might not see again he asked, ' Could you kiss me? ' and you bent down and kissed him. Well, I'm that major and I say, God bless you for all your kindness! "

God bless Mrs. Livermore, repeated thousands of voices through all the North.

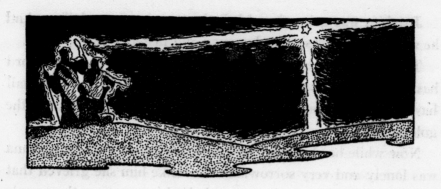

THE GREATEST MARY OF THEM ALL

Mary the Virgin: c. 12 B. C.—48 or 63 A. D.

A VERY long time ago in a far-away country in the western part of Asia, in a village called Nazareth there lived a shepherd named Joachim with Anna his wife. And they were Jews, of the royal family of David.

Pure and righteous lives they led serving the Lord with all their hearts. They were exceeding rich with great fields and herds of cattle and flocks of sheep and goats. Yet they were not happy, for they'd been married twenty years and had no children. This caused them sorrow and shame.

On one of the feast days of the Jews Joachim took to the temple at Jerusalem a double offering. But the priest said, " I cannot accept your gift."

The shepherd looked at him in astonishment.

" I must refuse it, because you have no sons or daughters."

187

Joachim was grieved and left the temple sorrowfully. And he went into the desert and prayed and fasted for forty days.

Then an angel came to him and said, " Joachim, the Lord has heard your prayer. Go down now, for you and Anna shall have a child. And this is the sign—she will meet you at the golden gate."

Now while her husband was gone for those forty days Anna was lonely and very sorrowful too. Like him she grieved that they had no child to take away their shame among the people and to banish the desolate quiet of their house. And she went into the garden and prayed earnestly that God would grant their wish and send them a child, as he did to Sarah and Abraham.

Suddenly an angel stood by her and said, " Anna, Anna, the Lord has heard your prayer. You shall have a child who shall be spoken of in all the world."

And she answered gratefully, " If it be a man-child or a maid, I will bring it as a gift unto the Lord to serve him in holy things."

Happy Anna went to greet her husband. And they met at the golden gate. Again Joachim took an offering to the temple. Now the priest accepted it. And what the angel told them came true. They had a little girl and they named her Mary.

Does this seem a queer way to tell you her story, when it sounds a little like the Bible and something like a fairy tale?

Well, this account of Mary's birth is only a tradition though she herself is a real person in history. But the record is very scant. During the two or three centuries after she lived a world of legends grew up about her. And though they weren't included in the Bible the priests made use of them to teach beautiful lessons to the people.

Of course we know that the eight stories where Mary is mentioned in the Bible verses are true. We know that the legends aren't true history. But some of them are very lovely, full of poetry and beauty. Perhaps they can teach you something too. And as I tell you about this Mary you'll recognize part as being in the New Testament, stories you already know by heart; and mixed in with these you'll find the old stories and traditions of the early church.

When she was three years old, to go on with the legend, Mary's parents took her to the temple at Jerusalem to keep Anna's vow and give her to the Lord. They placed her on the lowest step while they changed their stained traveling garments for clean and fitting dress. Quite alone, not once turning back the child went up the fifteen marble steps to the altar.

At that moment the high priest left the temple service. He came out and stood at the top of the steps to receive her. He kissed her and said, " Mary, in thee the Lord will show his redemption to the children of Israel." And all the people loved her.

With the other virgins Mary lived in the temple. Their time was spent in praying and singing psalms, in learning the

Jewish law and the old prophecies. They were taught to spin and weave and embroider. Of all the girls the little maid from Nazareth was most given to prayer. She knew more of God's law.

And as she grew in years Mary grew also in grace. She was humble and kind and modest. She was earnest and gentle, free from pride and deceit. She was as studious as she was industrious, as wise as she was chaste and pure. Like a dove she lived in the temple. And every day the angels brought her food and talked with her and kept her from all evil.

Now when the virgins were twelve or fourteen years old the high priest ordered them to return home to be married. For in Palestine it was the custom for girls to marry far younger than with us.

" But my parents," Mary said, " have given me to the Lord. Oh, I do not want to leave the temple! I have no wish to marry."

The priest was perplexed. He inquired of God what he should do.

" Summon to the house of the Lord," an angel directed, " all the marriageable men of Judah. Each one must bring his rod. By a sign the husband of Mary will be chosen."

With the rest came a carpenter named Joseph, of the family of David. The men handed their rods to the high priest who carried them into the temple. And having prayed he came back and returned them to their owners. Last of all he gave Joseph's. And behold! a dove dazzling white as the snow came out of the rod, lighted on the carpenter's head and then flew toward heaven.

Now here's another version of this story: All night the rods lay on the altar. And lo! in the morning the priest found Joseph's budded forth into leaves and pink flowers. Thus he was pointed out as the virgin's husband. And the disappointed suitors broke their rods in despair.

So Mary and Joseph were betrothed. The high priest himself joined their hands. On her finger the carpenter placed the ring—the very ring, tradition says, that your grandmother and I saw, and you'll see it some day, in the cathedral of Perugia, one of the hill towns of Italy.

The priests wanted a new veil for the temple. Seven maidens were selected to draw lots for the spinning and weaving of the different parts—the gold and green, the linen and silk, the blue, the scarlet and the purple. Remembering how skilled Mary was they sent to ask her to be one of the seven. And the purple, the color of royalty, fell to her lot.

While she was busy with this work she had a wonderful visitor, the angel Gabriel.

"Hail, Mary!" he greeted her. "The Lord is with thee. Blessed art thou among women."

In Latin this begins "Ave Maria," and the angel's words made one of the prayers of the early church. The ringing of the bell that we call the Angelus is named from the first word of this Bible story.

Mary was troubled till the angel said soothingly, "Fear not, for you have found favor with God." And he went on to give his message—that she'd been chosen to be the mother of Jesus, the Messiah for whom the Jews had been waiting for hundreds of years; that her son would sit on the throne of David to reign over the people; and of his kingdom there would be no end.

"How shall this be?" asked Mary wondering, her face full of a strange, new light.

"God's power shall overshadow you. And the child shall be called the son of God."

Awed by the message Mary bowed her head and answered humbly, " I am the handmaid of the Lord."

Gabriel said too that some time before he had been sent to tell Elizabeth that she would have a son. Mary decided to visit this cousin, though the distance from Nazareth to the hill country of Judea was more than a hundred miles. When she arrived Elizabeth suddenly recognized her as the future mother of Jesus.

"Blessed are you among women," she exclaimed, "and blessed is your child!"

And Mary as if inspired broke out into poetry, beautiful verses of praise and joy and happy thankfulness. You remember when we learned them together?

> " My soul doth magnify the Lord,
> And my spirit hath rejoiced in God my saviour."

The early church with its service in Latin used this as one of its hymns, calling it the Magnificat. And even when it's sung or read in English it's called the Magnificat still.

You can see how well Mary had studied in the temple, how thoroughly she knew the Jewish books of the law and the prophets. For in these few verses there are more than fifty expressions borrowed from the Old Testament. And Biblical phrases come into your speech only when you are very, very familiar with them and know them by heart.

How Elizabeth and Mary must have rejoiced as they shared their messages—these two women who were to be the greatest mothers in the world, their sons the greatest of prophets and the greatest of kings!

After three months the virgin returned to Nazareth. And Joseph took her to his own house rejoicing. But the child was not to be born there. For the Roman emperor who ruled over Palestine ordered all the people to go to their own towns to be enrolled for new tax records. Belonging to the family of David Joseph must go to his town of Bethlehem, and Mary with him.

There in a stable, because there was no room for them in the inn, Jesus was born. The child who was to reign over David's people was wrapped in swaddling clothes and laid in the manger. And the old legend says the ox and the ass bowed down to him while the place was filled with a great light, brighter than the sun.

The future king had visitors even the first night. The shepherds who watched their flocks heard from the angels the glad tidings of a saviour born that very day in David's city, and came to worship him. To Mary and Joseph they told the heavenly message. And the mother remembered all these things and pondered them in her heart.

To Jerusalem his parents took the baby Jesus to present him to the Lord. There devout old Simeon who had been told that he should live to see the Messiah, recognized the child as the redeemer of the world.

"Now I can depart in peace," said he.

Other visitors there were, wise men who had seen the star in the east and came to worship the new ruler of the Jews. How amazed the virgin was at the rich gifts they brought him—gold for the king and incense for the god and myrrh for the man condemned to die. Warned in a dream not to return to Herod, the jealous Roman governor who had directed them, they went home by another road.

And warned in a dream that Herod would try to kill Jesus to prevent the child's growing up to be king in his stead, Joseph and Mary and the baby fled at night and went to Egypt. A long journey it was through a desert country where there were many wild beasts. But by a miracle the way was shortened. Harmlessly lions and panthers played around the child.

The heat was so great that Mary begged to rest under a palm tree. Looking up she wished they could have some of the cool fruit, for all their water was gone.

"O tree, bend down your branches and refresh my mother with your fruit," said Jesus.

The tall palm bent down to the feet of the virgin. From its

JOSEPH AND MARY AND THE BABY FLED AT NIGHT

roots came a spring of water, clear and sparkling. When they were starting on their journey again the child turned to the tree.

"One of your branches shall be carried away by my angels to be planted in paradise. And to all who succeed in any contest men shall say, 'You've won the palm of victory!'"

While he was speaking an angel appeared, took up a branch and flew with it to heaven.

But Herod was not satisfied, says the legend, with sending his soldiers to kill all the young children in Bethlehem. When he discovered that Joseph and Mary had fled he sent officers to pursue them. The fugitives went by a field where a man was sowing.

"If anyone asks you," said the virgin, "whether we've passed this way make answer, 'Yes, when I was sowing this wheat.'"

And behold, a miracle! In one night the seed sprang up into stalk and blade and ear, ready for the harvest. The next morning some Roman soldiers marching by called out, "Have you seen an old man with a woman and child traveling this way?"

"Yes," said the farmer busily reaping.

"How long since?

"When I was sowing this wheat," was the answer. And in great wonder he saw them turn back and give over their pursuit.

The old legend goes on to tell that when the party arrived in Egypt the three hundred idols in the temple there fell to the ground and were broken in pieces. The priests found them lying on their faces though only Mary and the child had been there.

For some months, perhaps years, the family stayed in Egypt until they heard of the death of Herod. Then they returned to Nazareth.

All too brief is the Bible story of this time while Mary waited for the promises to come true. Year by year she saw her son grow in body and spirit, filled with wisdom, the grace of God upon him. With hope and fear, with joy and pity she watched over him. He was a sacred charge, hers for a short while, to be trained for a great work. So carefully educated a mother, you may be sure, would teach her son the Jewish books of the law and the prophets. Did she tell him when reading of the coming of the Messiah that he was the one referred to so frequently?

Each year Joseph and Mary went to Jerusalem for the celebration of the passover. When he was twelve years old they took Jesus with them. The feast days over they started back with the company from Nazareth. They did not notice that the boy remained in the city. Thinking he was with some friends they did not look for him till the first day's journey was ended.

Anxiously they searched. Anxiously they returned to Jerusalem. Not till the third day did they find him in the temple listening to the learned doctors of the law, asking questions and astonishing them all with his replies.

" Why have you done this? " asked Mary. " We've searched for you in sorrow."

And when he answered, "Why did you look for me? There's no place where I'd so surely be as in my Father's house," neither Joseph nor Mary understood what he meant. This too the mother kept in her heart.

But he was not to leave her yet. A dutiful, obedient lad he returned to Nazareth. His wisdom increased with his years. With both God and man he grew in favor. Soon after this visit to Jerusalem Joseph must have died since the Bible and the legends mention him no more. And in the little house at Nazareth lived Mary and her son, he I suppose a carpenter like Joseph and she busy with her household.

As she wove for him the robe made without a seam, which miraculously grew with his growth, she often thought of Gabriel's message and of the wise men and of the king her son would be. How hateful the rule of Rome was to the people! The taxes were so heavy! Constantly they were reminded of their masters—Roman laws and Roman soldiers and Roman money. And always the Jews hoped for the redeemer whose coming had been foretold, who would throw off this bondage and make them once more a glorious nation.

Did Mary perhaps remember what the high priest and Simeon had said when at thirty Jesus left home to teach and preach to the people? Was this the beginning of the prophecy's fulfilment, his baptism among sinners at the Jordan? Hard it was to let him go. But she listened with pride when she heard of great crowds that followed him about, of marvelous healings he made just by touching some sick man with his hands or by bidding him rise and walk, and of the parables of common, every-day things by which he taught his lessons.

Once Mary went to Capernaum to persuade him to return home for a rest. She found him surrounded by a throng of people, so many that she could not get near. She sent in word that she was there and wished to speak with him.

"Who is my mother," was his strange reply, "and who are my brothers? Those who do the will of my Father in heaven are my brother and sister and mother."

This was as strange as the answer the twelve-year-old boy had made in the temple, or his reply at the wedding feast at Cana when at her request he turned the water into wine.

Hard it was that Mary could not share his career and his glory, that she heard only rumors of his miracles—of his stilling the tempest, his feeding thousands of people with five loaves and two small fish, and making blind men see. But if he were to be a great king how came it that his disciples were such humble folk, common fishermen? Why was it that the sick on whom he used his gift of healing were outcast lepers and blind beggars, not often a daughter of Jairus or a centurion's son?

Why did the great ones of the Jewish world, the Pharisees and the priests, hold aloof and refuse to follow him? Yes, in scorn and hatred they held aloof, in envious fear of the growing popularity of this carpenter's son. More and more, report said, Jesus spoke of his death. Nearer and nearer came the shadow of the cross.

The disciples told Mary of their last supper with her son. She learned of the tragic scene in the garden when the Roman soldiers arrested him. She knew the mockery of the trials before high priest and Pilate and Herod. As she listened to John's report, in her ears dinned the mad shouts of the people, " Give us not this man, but Barabbas! "—Barabbas who was guilty of murder.

" Crucify him! " cried the fickle crowd who had listened so eagerly to his teaching, who only a few days before had welcomed him with palm branches and hosannas. When she heard that the sentence was confirmed Mary's heart was wellnigh broken.

Yet her mother love never failed. All the way to Calvary she followed. She watched while the body of her son was fastened to the cross and he suffered there. A king, they had said. And now he was dying. If she had only known that his reign was beginning!

In the darkness that came over the land at noon Mary stood near the foot of the cross while the passers-by reviled Jesus and the soldiers cast lots for his seamless coat. She heard him speak about his great thirst, heard him promise pardon to a thief and beg forgiveness for his enemies. Again he broke the silence remembering her while he redeemed the world,

"Woman, behold thy son!" and to John the disciple whom he loved, "Behold thy mother!"

With sublime faith and fortitude Mary stood by till the end. Then going home with John she waited in grief and hope till there came the glorious news that Jesus had risen from the dead. Frequent stories of his appearing to his followers she heard, then of his ascension into heaven. With the disciples in that upper room in Jerusalem she waited for the coming of the Holy Spirit. There the Bible story leaves her.

But the old legends building on to that account tell of Mary's later years. Beloved by everyone she lived in the house of John on Mount Sion. Her days were spent in visiting the places made sacred by the life and death of her son. She was an example to all women. She encouraged the early Christians.

One day while she was praying at the tomb of Jesus an angel appeared holding a palm branch gathered in paradise. "In three days," was the message he brought, "you will enter heaven."

Mary longed to see the disciples once more. From all parts of the world they were caught up in clouds and brought, tradition says, to that same upper chamber where she had waited with them. A mighty sound filled the house. A delicious perfume spread through the room. She heard the disciples singing a hymn. She heard the answer of angel voices, "Alleluia!"

"My soul doth magnify the Lord," she began, "and my spirit hath rejoiced——" Repeating the Magnificat she died.

Three virgins were chosen to prepare Mary's body. But

such a glory of light surrounded it that touching it they could not see it. Reverently the disciples carried it to a new tomb in the garden of Gethsemane. John walked first carrying the palm branch from paradise. For three days voices were heard praising the risen Jesus.

Welcomed by troops of angels blowing their silver trumpets and touching their silver lutes Mary was seated beside her son as queen of heaven, the virgin who had woven the royal purple for the veil of the temple.

But one of the disciples was far away in India and arrived too late. Bitterly Thomas wept because he could not see Mary once more.

" Come with us," said Peter and John, " to her tomb."

The three men rolled away the stone. Instead of the body they found lilies and roses, the symbols of purity and love. Looking up Thomas saw the virgin in a glory of light. To reassure him she flung down to him her girdle.

Departing to the far east Thomas gave her precious gift to one of his followers at Jerusalem. For a thousand years it was hidden from the eyes of the world. A prized inheritance, its care descended from father to son.

During the crusades an Italian from the town of Prato lodged with the custodian of the girdle and fell in love with his beautiful daughter. She returned to Italy with him taking the virgin's gift as her dowry. It's still kept in the cathedral of Prato and every year is carried in procession through the streets—you'll see it just as we did that beautiful May day.

The little house in Nazareth where Mary was born and where she received Gabriel's message was carefully preserved for many years. When the Turks ruled over Palestine there was great danger that it might be destroyed or profaned. So four angels lifted it up and carried it over land and sea to a grove in Loretto, a village in Italy. And there it is to-day encased in white marble, a favorite place of pilgrimage.

These are some of the legends of the virgin Mary. Very, very popular they were long years ago before there were many books. Where nowadays religion speaks to us through printed words, then it was by pictures, the books of the ignorant. But to read those books you must understand the language in which they're written.

In the many paintings of Mary you'll find all the legends and Bible stories—the angel appearing to Joachim and to Anna, the virgin in the temple and her betrothal, and Thomas with the girdle as well as the coming of the shepherds and the wise men from the east. And if you know both the legends and the Gospel account a new world of enjoyment will come to you in the pictures.

Not one of their details is without a meaning. When you see Mary with a lily or rose, you know what it stands for. But the star, the book, the palm and olive, the globe or pomegranate, her red tunic and blue mantle, each has a special meaning too. Some time you'll learn the whole story. Wouldn't you like to make a collection of this Mary's pictures? For fifteen hundred years the greatest artists of the world have painted her with an ideal face full of sweet earnestness and a calm, glad beauty.

Indeed in all history there's no woman so honored. Painters and sculptors, poets and musicians and architects and humble laborers have joined in giving their best work—verse or music or beautiful chapel—to pay her special honor. The churches dedicated to her the world over are counted by the thousand. On the banners of mediæval emperors, on the standard of Jeanne d'Arc her likeness and name were carried into battle. The Bible verses about her are now a part of the daily service in Greek and Roman and English church.

And to people everywhere whatever their faith or creed, this Mary is the ideal of womanhood pure and holy, of sweet and tender motherhood. Her humility, her tender sympathy and wisdom, her great heart of love and pity are not only for those who worship and adore her, but for all of us to think about, to ponder in our hearts.

And especially you who bear her name should try to be like her and daily say, " My soul doth magnify the Lord," and daily listen for the angel's greeting, " Mary, the Lord is with thee."

Edward Shenton